HYPNOTHERAPY TEACHING, TRAINING AND SUPERVISION

Jacquelyne Morison

Jacquelyne Morison Publishing

All material © Jacquelyne Morison 2017 unless otherwise stated. The right of Jacquelyne Morison to be identified as the author of this work has been asserted by her in accordance with the Copyright, Designs and Patents Act 1988.

All rights reserved. Except as permitted under current legislation no part of this work may be photocopied, stored in a retrieval system, published, performed in public, adapted, broadcast, transmitted, recorded or reproduced in any form or by any means without the prior permission of the copyright owner. All enquiries should be addressed to Jacquelyne Morison Publishing.

British Library of Cataloguing-in-Publication Data

A catalogue entry for this book is available from the British Library.

ISBN 978-0-9929973-4-2

Published in Cheltenham by Jacquelyne Morison Publishing 2017.

Contents

Teaching, Training & Supervision Overview — 1

- About the Book 3
- Teaching & Training the Practitioner 5
- Supervising the Practitioner 9

The Tutor & the Learner — 11

The Tutor 13
- Tutorial principles 13
- The tutorial role 13
- Personal attributes 14
- Professional attributes 16
- Personal motivation 17
- The tutor assignment 18

The Prospective Learner 21
- Understanding the prospective learner 21
- Background experience 23
- Innate intelligence 23
- Personality traits 24
- Personal aspirations 25
- The prospective learner assignment 26

The Learner 29
Understanding the adult learner 29
Learning potential 29
Perspective 30
Maturity 31
The learner assignment 32

Course Planning — 35

Learning Objectives 37
Compiling the learning objectives 37
Course objectives 37
Module objectives 38
Session objectives 39
Learning objectives evaluation 40
Learning objectives assignment 41

Course Programme 43
Compiling the course programme 43
Programme topics 44
Programme modules 46
Programme activity 48
Programme structure 51
Course programme evaluation 53
Course programme assignment 54

Course Synopsis 55
Compiling the course synopsis 55
Programme synopsis 55
Module synopsis 57
Course synopsis evaluation 60
Course synopsis assignment 60

Training Modules 61
Compiling the training module 61

Module topics	62
Module activity	63
Module structure	64
Training module evaluation	66
Training module assignment	67

TRAINING SESSIONS — 69

Compiling the training session	69
Session topics	69
Session activity	70
Session structure	72
Training session evaluation	73
Training session assignment	74

LEARNING PRINCIPLES — 75

LEARNING PSYCHOLOGY — 77

Learning psychology principles	77
Training delivery	78
Training activity	78
Learning psychology assignment	80

PROCESS-BASED EDUCATIONAL THEORY — 83

Process-based theory principles	83
Knowledge acquisition	84
Skill acquisition	85
Active learning	87
Passive learning	89
Process-based theory assignment	91

LEARNING-BASED EDUCATIONAL THEORY — 93

Learning-based theory principles	93
Behavioural learning	95
Cognitive learning	95
Affective learning	96

Self-awareness learning 97
Humanistic learning 98
Gestalt learning.. 98
Experiential learning 99
Learning-based theory assignment.. 100

CONTEXT-BASED EDUCATIONAL THEORY 103
Context-based theory principles.. 103
Human-communication learning... 105
Social-interaction learning 105
Environmental-engagement learning 106
Situational-activity learning.. 107
Critical-appraisal learning 107
Critical-reflection learning.. 108
Diversity learning 109
Constructivist-interaction learning 109
Group learning... 110
Individual learning 111
Context-based theory assignment.. 112

LEARNING STRATEGY... 115
Learning strategy principles.. 115
Active-engagement learning 116
Reflective learning 117
Theoretical learning 118
Experimental learning 118
Analogical learning 119
Perceptive learning 120
Imitative-practice learning 120
Learning strategy assignment... 121

LEARNER MOTIVATION 123
Learner motivation principles 123
Intrinsic motivation... 124
Aspirational motivation 125

Social motivation 125
Learner motivation assignment 126

LEARNER NURTURING **129**
Learner nurturing principles 129
Trainee rapport 129
Trainee championing 130
Trainee challenging 131
Trainee collaboration 131
Learner nurturing assignment 132

LEARNER ASSESSMENT **135**
Learner assessment principles 135
Informal assessment 136
Formal assessment 137
Assessment methodology evaluation 137
Learner assessment assignment 138

TEACHING PRINCIPLES 141

TEACHING PSYCHOLOGY **143**
Teaching psychology principles 143
Theoretical-practical teaching 144
Active-passive teaching 145
Teaching psychology assignment 147

TEACHING STRATEGY **149**
Teaching strategy principles 149
Episodic teaching 150
Continuous teaching 151
Trainee-centred teaching 152
Curriculum-centred teaching 153
Informal teaching 153
Formal teaching 154
Teaching strategy evaluation 154

Teaching strategy assignment 155

Teaching Methodology 157
Teaching methodology principles 157
Group presentation 159
Group demonstration 160
Group discussion 162
Group questioning 163
Supervised practice 164
Project-work 166
Teaching methodology assignment 167

Teaching Resource Utilization 169
Teaching resource utilization principles 169
Audio-visual equipment 171
Presentation equipment 172
Internet resources 174
Handout material 174
Teaching resource utilization assignment 176

Teaching Theory Application 179
Teaching theory application principles 179
Learning intentions 181
Topic presentation 182
Practical guidelines 183
Tangible outcomes 183
Trainee performance 184
Trainee feedback 185
Teaching standards 185
Teaching theory application assignment 186

Teaching Programme Evaluation 189
Teaching programme evaluation principles 189
Learner evaluation 191
Learning objective evaluation 192

Teaching methodology evaluation 193
Teaching programme evaluation assignment................................194

TEACHING & LEARNING MODELS 197
Teaching-learning models 197
Basic teaching model..197
Cycle of learning experience model 199
Anthroposophical teaching model 201
Teaching and learning models assignment 203

SUPERVISORY PRINCIPLES   205

THE SUPERVISOR 207
Supervisory principles 207
The supervisory role..207
Supervisory attributes 208
The supervisor assignment 209

SUPERVISORY ENQUIRY 211
Supervisory enquiry principles 211
Practice methodology..212
Supervisee's professional status 212
Client's psychological status 213
Supervisory enquiry assignment 215

SUPERVISORY GUIDANCE 217
Supervisory guidance principles 217
Supportive guidance..218
Mentoring guidance 219
Inspirational guidance...220
Developmental guidance...221
Supervisory guidance assignment 222

PRACTICE METHODOLOGY 225
Practice methodology principles 225

vii

Psychodynamic methodology 228
Humanistic methodology 228
State-oriented methodology 229
Transpersonal methodology 230
Biodynamic methodology 230
Cognitive methodology 231
Behavioural methodology 232
Practice methodology assignment 233

PRACTICE APPROACH 235

Practice approach principles 235
Cause-resolution approach 236
Effect-resolution approach 236
Emotive-focus approach 237
Cognitive-focus approach 237
Treatment strategy 238
Environmental factors 240
Practice approach assignment 241

SUPERVISORY PRACTICE 243

SUPERVISEE-CLIENT INTERACTION 245

Supervisee-client interaction principles 245
Supervisee perspective 246
Client perspective 248
Supervisee-client interaction assignment 249

SUPERVISEE-CLIENT PHENOMENA 251

Supervisee-client phenomena principles 251
Client-projection 253
Client-transference 253
Client-attachment 255
Supervisee counter-projection 257
Supervisee counter-transference 257

Supervisee counter-attachment 259
Supervisee-client phenomena assignment 260

SUPERVISORY STYLE 263
Supervisory style principles 263
Formative style 264
Restorative style 265
Collegiate style 265
Authoritative style 266
Supervisory strategy 266
Supervisory style assignment 268

SUPERVISORY APPROACH 271
Supervisory approach principles 271
Three-phase approach 273
Seven-phase approach 274
Supervisory approach assignment 276

SUPERVISORY ORGANIZATION 279
Supervisory organization principles 279
Individual supervision 280
Group supervision 280
Supervisory group conduct 282
Supervisory group style 283
Supervisory organization assignment 285

SUPERVISORY MODELS 287
Supervision models 287
Psychodynamic supervision 289
Client-centred supervision 289
Supervisee-centred supervision 289
Matrix-centred supervision 290
Person-centred supervision 290
Cognitive-behavioural supervision 291
Integrated-development supervision 291

Tiered-development supervision 292
Supervisory models assignment 292

APPENDICES 295

FURTHER READING 297

INDEX 301

ABOUT JACQUELYNE MORISON 307

Teaching, Training & Supervision Overview

ABOUT THE BOOK

Hypnotherapy Teaching, Training and Supervision has been designed to provide the hypnotherapy trainer and supervisor with a handy reference tool.

This book does not wish to impose a prescriptive set of principles for hypnotherapy teaching and supervisory practice but instead it contains some viable and practical guidelines for working in a dynamic and organically evolving profession.

Any tutor – whether qualified and experienced or a mere fledgling in training – can, of course, always benefit from some additional guidance and advice about how to do the job. *Hypnotherapy Teaching, Training and Supervision* will hence constitute worthwhile reading for those who are involved in the training and the nurturing of the hypnotherapy professional.

Teaching & Training the Practitioner

The education and supervision of practitioners in the professional hypnotherapy sector is a flourishing enterprise and the profession will undoubtedly continue to propagate.

In the UK alone the General Hypnotherapy Standards Council (GHSC), for instance, which is the largest and most prominent professional body for assessing and validating hypnotherapy training, has accredited over 240 professional training organizations during the last 15 years with around 140 currently listed. All these training providers offer, or have previously offered, practitioner training with many establishments also providing continuing professional development courses.

Training school registrants of the GHSC represent not only the UK but also Australia, Bulgaria, Canada, the Channel Islands, France, Greece, Iceland, Hong Kong, India, Malaysia, Singapore, Slovenia, South Africa, Spain and Thailand.

Professional training establishments worldwide offer hypnotherapy courses for prospective practitioners in the full spectrum of psychological approaches – encompassing psychodynamic, humanistic, transpersonal and cognitive-behavioural disciplines.

The remit of the GHSC is to monitor the standards of training school registrants, to protect the wellbeing of the public who use their services and to promote hypnotherapy as a legitimate and ethical profession. The GHSC also publishes a Professional Code of Ethics for practitioners and operates a formal Complaints and Disciplinary Procedure in order to ensure client safety and practitioner accountability.

The General Hypnotherapy Register (GHR), which comes under the umbrella of the GHSC, has registered in excess of 6,500 UK-based individual practitioners during the last 16 years as well as practising hypnotherapists in over 40 other countries with well in excess of 3,000 practitioners currently listed.

There are, of course, other training organizations which offer hypnotherapy training under their own umbrella which sit outside the voluntary-registration schemes in the UK because no formal state-registration policy exists.

Hypnotherapy tutors differ in terms of their own professional training from the tutor who already possesses teaching qualifications and training experience to the instructor who has merely learned on the job and has become proficient by this means. The hypnotherapy teaching professional, of course, is not necessarily one with a long string of impressive paper qualifications because all teachers are born and reared rather than manufactured.

SUPERVISING THE PRACTITIONER

Clinical supervision will be an essential and integral part of the hypnotherapist's professional development and career enhancement programme.

Supervisory assistance will also be a natural adjunct to the training process and will encourage the newly qualified practitioner to become a fully rounded working professional.

Supervisory work may include meetings with colleagues or sessions with a clinical supervisor on a one-to-one basis as well as course attendance, background reading and relevant research in order to keep abreast of any current developments within the profession and to maintain an awareness of closely related professions.

The GHSC stipulates categorically as a condition of registration that the practitioner should endeavour to maintain and to improve his existing skills with a view to both professional furtherance and personal development.

Receiving supervision, therefore, will enhance both the practitioner's work and the outcome of his client's therapeutic encounter.

The Tutor & the Learner

THE TUTOR

TUTORIAL PRINCIPLES

You might first need to appreciate what teaching entails and what your tutorial role will be during the learning experience for your trainee.

Essentially teaching will be a means of organizing and managing the learning environment and the teaching resources in order to maximize your trainee's learning potential. This concept can be further illustrated by considering your tutorial role in the teaching-learning equation.

THE TUTORIAL ROLE

Your role as a tutor will be one of planning and preparation prior to the commencement of your formal training delivery followed by the live management of the learning process for your course-participants.

You will, consequently, be responsible for planning, organizing and delivering teaching and, in the process, you will maximize the innate learning potential of your trainee who will be receiving your tuition in order to acquire skill and knowledge.

Your tutorial role will be akin to that of an orchestral conductor. The conductor of the orchestra will be in overall command of and responsible for the artistic presentation of the musical work while the musicians are still professionals who are able to take considered decisions in their own right yet they all tacitly agree to be directed by an independent party.

PERSONAL ATTRIBUTES

As a tutor of hypnotherapy practitioners you will need, above all, to be true to yourself and to be happy in your own skin.

In order to aspire to this idyllic state you should undertake some form of in-depth investigative personal therapy so that you can exorcize your demons. A methodology which can address root-cause analysis and resolution, such as psychodynamic analytical hypnotherapy, will, of course, be the most efficient way of achieving this aim.

A hefty dose of personal therapy will buoyantly sustain you very effectively through all the trials and tribulations of teaching. With a belt-and-braces approach to your own personal therapeutic journey you will be well equipped to understand the way in which the human mind operates. You will also be well placed to gauge the way in which your trainee's psyche will function and see the way in which he will be unravelling his emotional upheaval during his learning experience.

In-depth personal therapy will, furthermore, allow you to gain an inherent understanding of client-transference and supervisee counter-transference manifestations. With this wisdom within your soul you will skilfully be able to circumvent any difficulties with group psychodynamics when one of your trainees experiences a bumpy ride.

While you may not be afraid of hard work and you may be dedicated to the task of assisting others some self-investigative therapy will also safeguard you from running yourself into the ground with over-dedication to duty. Excessive work can so easily become the lot of the tutor who might wish to sacrifice his own needs in the service of others. You should learn, consequently, how to care for yourself while undertaking any form of teaching in which helping others will be the primary aim.

By ridding yourself of your own emotional hang-ups and resolving your stressful-traumatic past, therefore, you will become richly endowed with the endless patience, the infinite flexibility and the sincere caring instincts which will be such vital commodities when teaching and training others.

You may also benefit personally from regular supervisory sessions – as an adjunct to your own personal therapy – in order to assist you with any hitches which you might encounter with your training group.

Professional attributes

You should possess a sizeable chunk of practice experience in order to teach your subject-matter so that you can speak with the voice of wisdom.

As a teacher you should be able to delve deeply into your subject-matter in order to carefully analyse the content before breaking this information down into bite-sized chunks so that it can be imparted piecemeal to your trainees.

You will need, therefore, to analyse every hypnotherapeutic technique and practice theory in detail so that you will understand fully what you wish to impart to your trainees. Each component part of a skill in the use of a given therapeutic technique, for instance, will need to be condensed into discrete steps so that your trainees can acquire that skill in manageable amounts until its application as a whole has become automatic.

As a tutor will you also need to be able to assess both your trainee's potential and his overall progress throughout your course. A comprehensive knowledge of your trainee as a person and as a learner, therefore, will be a vital part of your work as a tutor.

Personal motivation

So that your teaching can be effective your tutorial role should begin with a degree of self-examination and an appraisal of your personal motivation.

Some preliminary self-enquiry will usefully help you to understand yourself and your personal motivation to become a teacher. You could, therefore, pose a number of questions in order to allow yourself to identify your motives and to ensure that you are travelling a road which will provide you with fulfilling job-satisfaction.

Searching questions should receive an honest answer so that you do not indulge in any form of self-deception. The list of possible self-searching questions can never be exhaustive if you undertake the self-examination process diligently and responsibly. Answering some typical self-examination questions in a quiet and relaxed state will provide you with a reliable answer about your mission and your motivation to teach.

Questions of a soul-searching nature will endeavour to highlight certain aspects of your psyche with reference to the teaching profession. You will discover, for instance, whether you possess an unrealistic aspiration to be an over-the-top do-gooder or whether you are harbouring any false illusions about the teaching profession being a money-spinning cushy number.

From this form of internal enquiry – provided that you are truthful with yourself – you will hence discover whether you are ideally suited to a profession which can guarantee hard work but with the reward of job-satisfaction and self-fulfilment.

THE TUTOR ASSIGNMENT

Answer the questions shown below about the tutor, pose any further questions which might arise during this process and decide what action, if any, you propose to take as a result of your findings.

- Why do you want to teach hypnotherapy?
- Do you want to teach under your own umbrella or for an established training organization?
- Can you appreciate the breadth of life experience which you will bring to your teaching?
- Would you be happier teaching an individual rather than a group of trainees?
- Would you prefer to teach a small group of trainees rather than having to cope with a large mass of course-participants?
- Do you want to teach for the sake of job-satisfaction or do you believe that you will make a considerable amount of money for very little effort?

- Are you really dedicated to the teaching profession and do you feel that you are on a mission to change the world?
- Do you believe that you will benefit more clients by teaching others to become hypnotherapy professionals?
- Do you find any aspect of hypnotherapy teaching daunting?
- Do you have any issues with performance anxiety?

The Prospective Learner

Understanding the Prospective Learner

It will be vital for you to understand your prospective learner so that you will know how to approach your group-participants and be guided towards organizing effective and appropriate teaching activity.

You might be advised, therefore, to personally interview each prospective trainee – either in person, via a video-conferencing system or simply over the telephone – before agreeing to enrol him on one of your training courses. This interviewing approach will also reinforce your caring role in the eyes of your future trainee.

When informally interviewing any prospective trainee you will, of course, need to outline your course objectives and possibly to give a flavour of the type of learning activity which will be undertaken on your course. Your prospective trainee can then make an informed choice about whether your course will meet his requirements.

You will need to consider the background, the intelligence-level and the personality traits of any prospective candidate in order to assess his suitability to become a member of the hypnotherapy profession or to join one of your continuing professional development courses.

You should be able to assess your prospective trainee's ultimate potential after an initial interview. You should be able to gain an overall impression of his current psychic state and thus estimate how much psychological distress he may have had to endure during in his life. You may also wish to point out the need for personal therapy – particularly for any course with a psychodynamic focus or one in which root-cause resolution will be sought – in order to gauge your applicant's reaction to such a stipulation.

Once you have received an overall awareness of your applicant you can then assess his learning potential so that you can later monitor his progress and his personal development accordingly.

Background experience

You may wish to discover what past experience of hypnotherapy your future trainee possesses so that you can appreciate his current level of knowledge.

Your prospective trainee for a practitioner course, for instance, will probably have some experience of being a client. A positive therapeutic outcome may, indeed, be responsible for prompting your prospective learner to actually become a practitioner. If your prospective trainee has limited experience of hypnotherapy then it may be incumbent on you to question his motivation for desiring to enter the hypnotherapy profession. You may then need to gauge the way in which you can bridge your applicant's knowledge-gap in due course.

When interviewing a prospective trainee for a continuing professional development course you would be advised to obtain details of his previous training and his experience as a practitioner.

Innate intelligence

So that you can plan an effective training programme it will be necessary for you to assess the innate intelligence of your prospective learner.

Innate intelligence has nothing whatsoever to do with paper qualifications, success in other fields or any similar accomplishments but it will be an inherent ability to think clearly and logically and to apply knowledge in a variety of circumstances.

When interviewing your prospective trainee it should become abundantly clear to you whether or not he has a basic level of innate intelligence. The likelihood will be that your prospective trainee will have an inherent aptitude, however, because the hypnotherapy profession will demand this ability and will only normally attract those of a certain level of intellect.

Personality traits

You will need to be assured that your future trainee will already possess the necessary personal attributes for joining the ranks of the caring profession.

Your prospective trainee should, therefore, exhibit qualities of integrity, trustworthiness, openness and sincerity in order to be a suitable candidate for the hypnotherapy profession. If your prospective trainee might cause you any degree of uncertainty about his suitability for practitioner training then it may be wise for you to decline him as a course-participant.

Your prospective trainee – like everyone else in the world – will obviously display certain neurotic tendencies but you will need to be assured in your own mind that such traits will naturally diminish after receiving some personal therapy.

You might also note the general outlook of your applicant in terms of his typical beliefs and his convictions about hypnotherapeutic intervention and, indeed, about life in general.

Any strong negative feelings about the way in which the world ticks, for instance, may be an impediment to ethical practice unless such beliefs can be resolved effortlessly in the therapeutic context. A practitioner with strong beliefs about religion, upbringing or politics, moreover, may not be of service to his client – especially if he might seek to impose such views on him during his therapeutic encounter.

Personal aspirations

You might wish to assess your prospective trainee in terms of his future aspirations, his talents and his inclinations.

You could enquire about a possible career direction or a personal interest, for instance, in order to capitalize on the way in which your future trainee could develop on your training course.

A trainee with an interest in working with children or with a knowledge of metaphysical philosophy, for instance, should be well catered for and should be nurtured in this direction in order to capitalize on his desires.

The prospective learner assignment

Answer the questions shown below about the prospective learner, pose any further questions which might arise during this process and decide what action, if any, you propose to take as a result of your findings.

- Can you meet and informally assess your potential learner?

- Have you fully outlined your course objectives and your course format to your potential learner so that he will be able to make an informed decision about your training course?

- Could your potential trainee eventually become a suitable candidate to work in professional practice as a hypnotherapy practitioner?

- Does your potential learner have any relevant background experience on which he can capitalize during his learning process?

- Does your course applicant have an innate intelligence which will assist him during his learning process?

- Can you identify any positive personality traits which your prospective learner should acknowledge as part of his developmental mission?

- Has your potential trainee already had experience of hypnotherapy either as a client or as a practitioner?
- What other types of alternative therapy training has your prospective trainee undertaken previously?
- What has prompted your potential learner to undertake a training course with you?
- What might be your potential learner's future?

THE LEARNER

UNDERSTANDING THE ADULT LEARNER

Your role as a tutor will be to motivate your learner by understanding his needs and gauging his ability and then tailoring your teaching activity accordingly.

An adult learner will bring a number of personal attributes to the training environment of which you should be soundly aware.

LEARNING POTENTIAL

You will need to understand the learning ability and the individual capabilities of your trainee in order to exploit his learning potential and to cope with any of his inherent limitations.

You will need, therefore, to assess your learner in terms of what he can in reality achieve in order to be able to set your long-term training goals. From this standpoint you will, consequently, need to consider the background experience and the future aspirations of your learner. You will also need to assess your learner's innate intelligence, his comprehension-level and his maturity-level in order to be able to tailor your teaching methodology accordingly.

Once you have set your training objectives and then tailored your teaching activity to cater for your learner's potential you will also need to monitor his rate of progress and to make any appropriate modifications to your training programme as necessary.

Perspective

Your adult learner will have gained a perspective on life which will be far broader than the limited view of life which the child or the young person possesses. This wide breadth of experience should greatly assist your trainee's learning process.

A wide perspective on life will bring your trainee inner knowledge, personal insight and an understanding of others which can be a valuable asset for him as a therapeutic practitioner. Your adult learner will also undoubtedly possess a myriad of existing skills, talents, interests and aspirations all of which you should capitalize on in the training environment.

MATURITY

Your mature learner will undoubtedly be on a personal-growth path and, as a tutor, you can capitalize on this healthy state of being and you should nurture your learner accordingly. You should encourage your learner's personal growth, therefore, towards personal individuation, learning independence and natural maturity throughout your training programme.

Your adult trainee will usually be engaged in the optimization of his potential and, therefore, his intrinsic motivational desire to learn should be high. You will, nevertheless, still need to stimulate and to maintain his interest even though you can usually capture his attention without undue effort.

Your mature learner will usually be highly motivated in terms of his personal goals, his career intentions and his expectation of a successful outcome during his learning experience. Your teaching activity should, therefore, promote autonomous self-discovery for your adult trainee. Your mature trainee will usually be self-referential and he will, therefore, be able to take responsibility for his own progress, development, self-assessment and self-directed learning activity.

Your adult learner should be able to make sound value-judgements about himself and others. You should, of course, endeavour to ensure that your learner's judgements about himself are realistic and not neurotically-driven. Your trainee, for example, may have an unhealthily over-inflated view of others and correspondingly he may retain an overly humble opinion of himself as a result.

THE LEARNER ASSIGNMENT

Answer the questions shown below about the learner, pose any further questions which might arise during this process and decide what action, if any, you propose to take as a result of your findings.

- Do you believe that you fully understand the needs of each of your trainees?
- What do you think might be the true learning potential of your trainee?
- Can you help your trainee to overcome any perceived or actual limitations to his learning ability?
- Would you consider that your trainee can successfully and effortlessly acquire and develop his practical skills?
- Will you need to adjust your teaching methodology in order to cater specifically for your learner?
- Can you successfully capitalize on your trainee's inherent skills, talents, interests and aspirations during his learning experience?

- In what ways might your learner's adult perspective on life be useful to him during his learning process?

- Does your trainee have the ability to be intrinsically self-motivated and self-directed so that he can organically evolve during his own learning experience?

- Can you help your trainee to perfect his skill so that he can achieve his maximum potential and, simultaneously, he can fulfil his personal aspirations?

- Does your trainee uphold any negative beliefs about his ability to acquire knowledge and skill which will need to be addressed in order to ensure that his learning experience will not be inhibited?

Course Planning

Learning Objectives

Compiling the learning objectives

Your teaching function will essentially be to manage the learning process so that your trainee can be placed in the most advantageous position in order to acquire theoretical knowledge and practical skill.

You will need to formulate a set of definitive learning objectives for each of your hypnotherapy training courses and then retain these aims in mind throughout your training programme.

Course objectives

For your hypnotherapy practitioner course it might be wise for you to devise a mission statement so that you will know well in advance what you hope your trainee will achieve and what he will be equipped for on qualification (see Figure 1: *Course Objectives*).

Your overall training course objective for a practitioner course will, in most cases, be to ensure that your trainee on graduation will have everything at his fingertips in connection with establishing and maintaining a thriving practice.

You might also wish to include the mission statement of your overall course objectives in your promotional material in order to ensure that your prospective trainee will be left in no doubt whatsoever about what to expect from your training course.

FIGURE 1: COURSE OBJECTIVES

HYPNOTHERAPY PRACTITIONER COURSE
10-weekend course
COURSE OBJECTIVES
Conduct hypnotherapy with a fee-paying client Set up in practice as a hypnotherapy practitioner

MODULE OBJECTIVES

For each individual module of your training programme you will need to appreciate precisely what you propose to cover with your trainee and to clearly identify what your intended module outcome will be as an integral part of your entire training programme (see Figure 2: MODULE OBJECTIVES).

An introductory module, for example, will probably include the basics of hypnotherapy practice by providing your trainee with information which explains hypnotic phenomenon and then allows him time for some practice sessions.

FIGURE 2: MODULE OBJECTIVES

INTRODUCTION TO HYPNOSIS MODULE
2-day module
MODULE OBJECTIVES
Appreciate the value of a hypnotic state for therapeutic relaxation
Induce a hypnotic state in a practice client
Encourage a deepened hypnotic state in a practice client
Compile and deliver a relaxation text to a practice client
Deliver a post-hypnotic suggestion to a practice client
Terminate a hypnotic state in a practice client

SESSION OBJECTIVES

For each individual training session which you propose to conduct you will need to formulate clear objectives for what you intend to teach, what will be expected of your trainee and what outcome you can both anticipate (see Figure 3: SESSION OBJECTIVES).

FIGURE 3: SESSION OBJECTIVES

	PAST-LIFE REGRESSION SESSION 90-minute session
SESSION OBJECTIVES	
Appreciate the use, value and application of past-life regression as a therapeutic tool Conduct a past-life regression therapy session with a practice client	

LEARNING OBJECTIVES EVALUATION

The planning of your entire course programme, the modular components and the individual training sessions will, of course, essentially be a theoretical exercise which you must continually evaluate for its effectiveness in practice.

You will, therefore, need constantly to review your plans – whether these be in written form or merely retained in your memory – in order to ensure that your training course can continue as a live and dynamic enterprise.

You may find that your learning objectives will need to be modified slightly – or even drastically – after delivering each training programme in the light of your accumulating teaching experience. This policy will keep your training course alive as an organically growing initiative.

Learning objectives assignment

Compile your learning objectives for your hypnotherapy practitioner course and your continuing professional development courses utilizing the template shown below for guidance.

Course/Module/Session Objectives
Duration
Course/Module/Session Objectives

COURSE PROGRAMME

COMPILING THE COURSE PROGRAMME

Your teaching function will be to undertake much in the way of preparatory work prior to actually delivering your training programme to your course-participants.

Your entire training course programme plan (also known as a *Syllabus* or a *Scheme of Work*) will need to be designed and structured so that individual training sessions can later be organized well in advance of your training delivery.

Your role as a tutor of hypnotherapy trainees will, almost certainly, be concerned with delivering tuition both to groups and to individuals and you will need to prepare for each of these scenarios.

It would be advisable for you to ensure that you build Into your training programme a significant degree of flexibility as circumstances might dictate in practice. Live training sessions will seldom go according to your plans and, therefore, it will be essential for you to cater for every unexpected eventuality. Time will need to be made up when you get behind schedule and spare time must occupied when you get ahead of yourself during your training delivery. Your training programme, consequently, must allow for any unscheduled contingency when your plan does not fit the live situation.

PROGRAMME TOPICS

Your course programme plan will initially consist of a basic list of course contents in terms of general topic headings (see Figure 4: PROGRAMME TOPICS).

You could start by making a rough list of training topics to be included on your course programme in higgledy-piggledy order which will subsequently be arranged chronologically. You will, by this means, be documenting your entire course content as the starting-point for all your planning activity.

Once your list of training topics has been compiled you will then need to decide how these topics can be grouped and prioritized in order to be able to format your training course into manageable units.

FIGURE 4: PROGRAMME TOPICS

HYPNOTHERAPY PRACTITIONER COURSE TOPICS	
PROGRAMME TOPICS	
Benefits of hypnosis	Deepeners
Ideomotor questioning	Client enquiries
Hypnotic induction	Client-centred approaches
Relaxation	Stress management
Guided visualization	Self-hypnosis
Evidence of hypnotic phenomena	Parts therapy
Time-line techniques	Examination nerves
Smoking cessation	Performance nerves
Fears and phobias	Suggestion
Weight management	Reframing
Confidence boosting	Metaphors
Ego-strengthening	Business development
Past-life regression	Practitioner confidence
Ethical practice	Client observation

Programme modules

Your preliminary list of course topics can now be suitably rearranged in a logical order and broken down into modular units in order to structure your entire course programme (see Figure 5: *Programme Modules*).

Your course programme should present your training themes arranged in sequence. Similar topics should, of course, be grouped together and fitted into the number of themed units of teaching which you will be delivering to your trainees. Those topics which you have already listed randomly, therefore, can now be arranged accordingly into topic groups. You may, of course, elect to make some amendments to your original list of topics during this process of modular design.

Figure 5: Programme Modules

HYPNOTHERAPY PRACTITIONER COURSE MODULES	
Topic	Learning Activity
Introduction to hypnosis	Hypnotic phenomena Benefits of hypnosis
Hypnotherapy basics	Hypnotic induction Evidence of hypnotic phenomena Suggestion Reframing

	Metaphorical imagery
	Deepeners
Client enquiries	Client note-taking
	Client observation
	Self-hypnosis
Relaxation and stress management	Relaxation scripts
	Guided visualization scripts
	Stress management techniques
Special therapeutic techniques	Ideomotor questioning
	Time-line techniques
	Client-centred approaches
	Parts therapy
Symptomatic resolution	Smoking cessation
	Fears and phobias
	Weight management
	Confidence boosting
	Ego-strengthening
	Past-life regression
	Examination and performance nerves
Hypnotherapy practice	Ethical practice
	Business development
	Practitioner confidence

Programme Activity

A training programme activity plan can greatly assist you by providing a list of topics broken down into theoretical learning and practical learning methodology categories as an adjunct to your modular plan (see Figure 6: *Programme Activity*)

Your training programme activity plan can allow you to take an overview of the way in which your course can be constructed effectively and might demonstrate the way in which you can allocate sufficient time for both theory and practice. A variant on this theme would show teaching activity, trainee activity and training resources as necessary.

Figure 6: Programme Activity

Hypnotherapy Practitioner Course Activity	
Theory	Practice
Course introduction History of clinical hypnosis Mesmer, Freud and Erickson Hypnotherapy practice Therapeutic process Analytical hypnotherapy Practitioner and client roles	Hypnotic induction, deepening and termination Self-hypnosis

Client note-taking Client assessment Client observation Fight-flight-freeze response Limbic system and vagus nerve	Metaphorical imagery
Analytical hypnotherapy overview Compliant client Cause and effect principles Investigation and resolution	Age regression Pinpointing Free association
Freudian psychodynamic theory Freud, Jung and Adler Psychoanalysis Analytical psychology Individual psychology	Imagery and symbolism Hypnotic art Inner child Inner advisor
Neo-Freudian psychodynamic theory Anna Freud, Klein, Mahler and Bowlby Object-relations theory Attachment theory	Ego-state therapy
Psychodynamic practice Memory processes Resistance Defensive strategies Transference and counter-transference	Past-life regression

Personality theories Freud, Jung and Fromm	
Humanistic psychology Rogers, Maslow, Frankl, May, Laing and Perls Client-centred therapy Existential therapy Gestalt therapy	Therapeutic re-enactment
Cognitive-behavioural therapy Beck, Glasser and Ellis Unconscious communication	Ideomotor questioning Belief restructuring Time-line Anchoring Dissociation Gold counselling
Therapeutic resolution Fight-flight-freeze symptoms Psychosomatic disorders Dysfunctional relationships Childhood abuse trauma	Treatment strategies Eclectic approaches
Therapeutic practice Practice promotion Clinical supervision Professional body registration	Brochure compilation Promotional planning

Programme Structure

Once your course programme modular plan has been completed you can now decide on the specific contents of each modular unit in order to provide an overall course structure (see Figure 7: PROGRAMME STRUCTURE).

You might find, for instance, that your course programme will lend itself naturally to becoming a number of weekend or week-long block sessions. Typically a hypnotherapy practitioner course may be broken down into a number of weekend or week-long modules.

Some topic units will fit nicely into one of your chosen blocks or, when necessary, items can be spread over a number of modular groups. When dealing with specific techniques or introducing ways of handling certain symptomatic patterns, for instance, you may find that several modular blocks will be required for a single topic group.

Figure 7: Programme Structure

\multicolumn{3}{c}{HYPNOTHERAPY PRACTITIONER COURSE STRUCTURE}
MODULE	TOPIC	LEARNING ACTIVITY
1	Introduction to hypnotherapy	Benefits of hypnosis Hypnotic induction Evidence of hypnotic phenomena

		Suggestion
		Reframing
		Metaphorical imagery
		Deepeners
2	Client enquiries	Client note-taking
		Client observation
		Self-hypnosis
3	Relaxation and stress management	Relaxation scripts
		Guided visualisation scripts
		Stress management techniques
4 – 5	Special therapeutic techniques	Ideomotor questioning methodology
		Time-line methodology
		Client-centred approaches
		Parts therapy methodology
6 – 11	Symptomatic resolution	Smoking cessation
		Fears and phobias
		Weight management
		Confidence boosting
		Ego-strengthening
		Past-life regression
		Examination and performance nerves

12	Hypnotherapy practice	Ethical practice
		Business development
		Practitioner confidence

Course programme evaluation

You will need constantly and regularly to evaluate your course programme plans in order to consider whether any changes could usefully be made after careful monitoring has taken place.

Whether any modifications to your course programme are slight or drastic will be a sign of the health of your training programme and so the evaluation process should be regarded by you as a positive benefit both for yourself and for your trainees.

Any adjustments which you choose to make to your overall course programme will, of course, need to be reflected in your course synopsis and will have a knock-on effect in terms of your plans for your training modules and your individual training sessions.

COURSE PROGRAMME ASSIGNMENT

Compile your course programme for your hypnotherapy practitioner course and your continuing professional development courses utilizing the template shown below for guidance.

		COURSE PROGRAMME PLAN	
			Duration
MODULE	TOPIC	THEORY	PRACTICE

COURSE SYNOPSIS

COMPILING THE COURSE SYNOPSIS

Once you have an overview of your entire course in the form of your completed course programme plan you can now extrapolate your course synopsis from this documented information.

Your course synopsis will primarily be designed as a promotional tool. Your course synopsis should provide the essence of your course objectives and your course content in order to allow your prospective trainee to take a considered decision about whether to enrol on your training course. Your course synopsis would, therefore, provide some insight into your training programme yet not contain any detailed analysis.

PROGRAMME SYNOPSIS

By focusing on the main modular topic themes you will easily be able to compile a course programme synopsis which you can then use for promotional purposes (see Figure 8: *Programme Synopsis*).

Your course programme synopsis could, if necessary, indicate the main modular units from your training programme in order to give your prospective trainee an idea of how your course content will be broken down.

FIGURE 8: PROGRAMME SYNOPSIS

HYPNOTHERAPY PRACTITIONER COURSE PROGRAMME SYNOPSIS
10 weekends over 1 academic year
COURSE SYNOPSIS
Introduction to hypnosis
Hypnotherapeutic methodology
Relaxation and stress management methodology
Special therapeutic methodology for ideomotor-questioning, time-line practice, client-centred approaches and parts therapy
Symptomatic resolution methodology for smoking cessation, fears and phobias, weight management, confidence boosting. ego-strengthening, past-life regression, performance nerves and examination nerves
Professional ethics in working practice
Practice promotion
Business establishment and maintenance

Module synopsis

Your module synopsis might be fleshed out from your course objectives and your course programme plan rather than being a bland statement of course contents as an overall course programme synopsis might (see Figure 9: *Module Synopsis*).

Figure 9: Module Synopsis

| **Hypnotherapy Practitioner Course Module Synopsis** ||
| *10 modular units* ||
Module	Content
Module 1	History of clinical hypnosis
	The work of Franz Mesmer, Sigmund Freud and Milton Erickson
	Hypnotherapy practice
	The therapeutic process
	The nature of analytical hypnotherapy
	The role of the practitioner and the client
Module 2	Case note-taking
	Client assessment
	Client observation
	The stress-trauma response
	The fight-flight-freeze response

	The role of the limbic system and the vagus nerve in the stress-trauma response
Module 3	Analytical hypnotherapy overview
	Need for client compliance
	Cause-and-effect principle of therapeutic resolution
	Investigative and resolution-focused approach
Module 4	Freudian psychodynamic theory
	The work of Sigmund Freud, Carl Jung and Alfred Adler
	Principles of psychoanalysis
	Principles of analytical psychology
	Principles of individual psychology
Module 5	Neo-Freudian psychodynamic theory
	The work of Anna Freud, Melanie Klein, Margaret Mahler and John Bowlby
	Principles of object-relations theory
	Principles of attachment theory
Module 6	Psychodynamic practice
	Memory processes
	Understanding unconscious resistance
	Understanding defensive strategies
	Principles of transference and counter-transference
	Personality theories
	Personality theories of Sigmund Freud, Carl Jung and Erich Fromm

Module 7	Humanistic psychology
	The work of Carl Rogers, Abraham Maslow, Victor Frankl, Rollo May, Ronald Laing and Fritz Perls
	Principles of client-centred practice
	Principles of existential therapy
	Principles of gestalt therapy
Module 8	Cognitive-behavioural therapy
	The work of Aaron Beck, William Glasser and Albert Ellis
	Principles of cognitive-behavioural practice
	Principles of unconscious communication
Module 9	Therapeutic resolution
	Fight-flight-freeze symptoms
	Psychosomatic-psychogenic disorders
	Dysfunctional relationships
	Childhood abuse stress-trauma
Module 10	Ethical therapeutic practice
	Practice promotion
	Clinical supervision
	Professional body registration

COURSE SYNOPSIS EVALUATION

You will need constantly and regularly to evaluate your course synopsis in order to ensure that what you publish about your course programme will accurately reflect your circumstances.

Whether any modifications to your course synopsis are slight or drastic will be a sign of the health of your training programme and so the evaluation process should be regarded by you as a positive benefit both for yourself and for your trainees.

COURSE SYNOPSIS ASSIGNMENT

Compile your course synopsis for your hypnotherapy practitioner course and your continuing professional development courses utilizing the template shown below for guidance.

	COURSE SYNOPSIS PLAN
	Duration
COURSE OBJECTIVES	
MODULE	**CONTENT**

Training Modules

Compiling the training module

Your course programme plan will often provide a guide to training modular content but now you will be able to plan in more detail the way in which each of your training modules will be constructed.

Within each of your training modules you should ideally aim to cover a complete subject area – although a number of short topics which are clearly related may also be expedient.

There should be a variety of learning activity for your trainee within each modular unit and, of course, ample practical work should be provided in order to enable his theoretical knowledge to be assimilated and transformed into practical skill which he can confidently apply in the workplace.

MODULE TOPICS

The topics to be included within any given training module are likely to be available in skeletal form in your overall course programme plan. Much of the selection work may already have been undertaken and, therefore, you will need simply to flesh out the bones of the information already in existence in your training programme plan.

When planning each of your training modules you will need to consider the total time allocated and then divide the modular content into discrete and manageable units.

When selecting topics you should ensure that each module will neither be overcrowded nor too skeletal and that each module has been well structured so as to form a viable entity in itself. If your modules are relatively short in length then one main topic may need to be split over one or more modular units. Short topics could similarly be grouped together within one module provided that the topics are related by some logical thread.

When selecting your module topics, therefore, you should endeavour to include items which have a natural affinity and can easily complement or dovetail into the entire module so that your trainee will feel a sense of continuity during his learning experience.

MODULE ACTIVITY

You could design your training module to include significant detail about teaching activity in terms of featuring both theoretical and practical components, tutor activity, learner activity and teaching resources (see Figure 10: MODULE ACTIVITY).

FIGURE 10: MODULE ACTIVITY

THERAPEUTIC RE-ENACTMENT MODULE	
	1-day module
MODULE OBJECTIVES	
Appreciate principles of gestalt methodology	
Acquire skill in therapeutic re-enactment methodology	
MORNING SESSION	
Recapitulate humanistic principles	Trainees describe humanistic principles
Distribute slide presentation handouts	Trainees observe slide presentation
Deliver slide presentation of gestalt therapy principles	Trainees make notes on handouts during slide presentation
BREAK	
Demonstrate therapeutic re-enactment methodology with a practice client	Trainees observe demonstration of therapeutic re-enactment methodology

Initiate discussion on ways of utilizing therapeutic re-enactment methodology	Trainees discuss possible ways of utilizing therapeutic re-enactment methodology
AFTERNOON SESSION	
Observe and monitor trainee practice	Trainees practice therapeutic re-enactment methodology
BREAK	
Supervise discussion of practice session feedback Invite questions as appropriate Summarize modular content	Trainees feedback practice sessions Trainees recapitulate and consolidate therapeutic re-enactment methodology

MODULE STRUCTURE

In many cases your training module structure will be an amalgam of your module objectives, your modular activity and an extrapolation from your course programme plan (see Figure 11: *MODULE STRUCTURE*).

FIGURE 11: MODULE STRUCTURE

INTRODUCTION TO HYPNOTHERAPY MODULE		
2-day module		
MODULE OBJECTIVES		
Appreciate the value of a hypnotic state for therapeutic relaxation Induce a hypnotic state in a practice client Encourage a deepened hypnotic state in a practice client Compile and deliver a hypnotic relaxation text to a practice client Deliver a post-hypnotic suggestion to a practice client Terminate a hypnotic state in a practice client		
DAY 1 MORNING		**DAY 2 MORNING**
Introduce self and trainees Introduce course, its structure, scope and overall objectives Distribute training materials Explain intrinsic value of hypnotherapy with case-study examples Elicit examples of hypnotherapy experience from trainees		Deliver a group hypnotic session utilizing induction, deepening, relaxation and termination methodology Distribute copies of a typical relaxation text Explain use of basic suggestion and post-hypnotic suggestion

Break	Break
Demonstrate hypnotic induction, deepening and termination methodology with a practice client Explain purpose of induction, deepening and termination procedure Elicit observable signs of hypnotic phenomena from trainees Invite questions	Ask trainees to compile a short hypnotic relaxation text Ask trainees to conduct a practice session using their compiled relaxation text
Day 1 Afternoon	**Day 2 Afternoon**
Ask trainees to practice simple hypnotic induction, deepening and termination methodology	Invite feedback from trainees on experience of hypnotic practice session as both client and practitioner
Break	Break
Invite feedback from trainees on experience of hypnotic practice session as both client and practitioner	Summarize modular content Invite questions Distribute homework assignment Deliver a group hypnotic session in order to consolidates learning

Training module evaluation

You will need constantly and regularly to evaluate all your training module plans in order to consider whether any changes could usefully be made as an ongoing process.

Whether any modifications to your training module plan are slight or drastic will be a sign of the health of your training programme and so the evaluation process should be regarded by you as a positive benefit both for yourself and for your trainees.

TRAINING MODULE ASSIGNMENT

Compile your training module plans for your hypnotherapy practitioner course and your continuing professional development courses utilizing the template shown below for guidance.

	TRAINING MODULE PLAN Duration
TRAINING MODULE OBJECTIVES	
DAY 1 MORNING	DAY 2 MORNING
BREAK	BREAK
DAY 1 AFTERNOON	DAY 2 AFTERNOON
BREAK	BREAK

TRAINING SESSIONS

COMPILING THE TRAINING SESSION

Your course programme plan and your modular content plan will very largely dictate the ingredients of each of the individual sessions which you will be required to conduct with your trainees.

A training session will essentially cover one single topic or even a sub-division of one main topic in order to fit into a relatively short space of time – perhaps merely an hour.

SESSION TOPICS

The topics to be covered within individual sessions will be contained in each of your training module plans. In planning a training session you will be concerned principally with the way in which your teaching will be delivered by perhaps elaborating on the details contained within your training module plans.

When planning your training sessions it will be essential for you to engage your learner in plentiful practical activity in order to stimulate and to maintain his interest while, simultaneously, directly involving him in the acquisition of a practical skill which he can apply outside the training environment. Your training session plan, therefore, should indicate a breakdown of both your teaching activity and the learning activity for your trainees so that you can clearly appreciate what both parties will undertake during the session.

While you may think that documenting a session plan will not be an essential activity because you can easily remember what will be required it may be useful, at least in principle, to have some form of written record to which you can refer in the future or which you can hand to another tutor for guidance.

Often your training session plan will cover only a part of the modular content because a training session will, of necessity, be confined to a limited period of uninterrupted and concentrated time. Several training sessions, therefore, may collectively need to be grouped together in order to cover one single topic on your course programme.

Session activity

Your training session plan (also known as a *Teaching-Learning Plan* or a *Lesson Plan*) will usually be an extrapolation of information contained in your training module compilation which has been adapted in order to show both teaching methodology and learning activity in context (see Figure 12: *Session Activity*).

Ideally your training session plan could, of course, also include information about teaching resources and learner assessment as well as any other relevant information which you might need to keep at hand.

FIGURE 12: SESSION ACTIVITY

INNER CHILD THERAPY SESSION PART I	
1-hour session	
SESSION OBJECTIVES	
Introduce trainees to the concept of working with the inner child	
TEACHING ACTIVITY	**LEARNING ACTIVITY**
Introduce concept of working with the inner child Question trainees about their knowledge and experience of inner child methodology Invite questions Explain the use of inner child rescue, protection, empowerment and nurturing methodology	Trainees cite previous knowledge and experience of working with the inner child Trainees make notes of inner child rescue, protection, empowerment and nurturing methodology Trainees discuss and offer suggestions for the use of inner child methodology Trainees plan an inner child methodology practice session

Invite suggestions for utilizing inner child methodology Oversee plans for an inner child practice session	

SESSION STRUCTURE

Your training session plan could usefully also indicate approximate timings for all your training activity (see Figure 13: *SESSION STRUCTURE*).

Your training session plan, therefore, could provide a detailed breakdown of teaching activity, learning activity, teaching resources, trainee assessment and timings so that you can at a glance see both the session content and the session structure.

FIGURE 13: SESSION STRUCTURE

IDEOMOTOR QUESTIONING SESSION PART 3
90-minute session
SESSION OBJECTIVES
Practice ideomotor questioning methodology Consolidate previous learning about ideomotor methodology

Teaching Activity	Learning Activity	Timing
Recapitulate principles of ideomotor questioning methodology Recapitulate yes/no answers only Recapitulate use fingers of dominant hand Recapitulate use of regression techniques Recapitulate use of resolution techniques	Trainees outline principles of ideomotor questioning methodology Trainees make notes on slide handouts	10
Monitor trainee question-construction	Trainees plan ideomotor questioning session and compile typical questions	15
Oversee trainee practice sessions	Trainees practice ideomotor questioning methodology	50
Evaluate practice sessions	Trainees feedback practice sessions	15

Training session evaluation

You will need constantly and regularly to evaluate all your training sessions in order to consider whether any changes could usefully be made as an ongoing process.

Whether any modifications to your training session plan are slight or drastic will be a sign of the health of your training programme and so the evaluation process should be regarded by you as a positive benefit both for yourself and for your trainees.

TRAINING SESSION ASSIGNMENT

Compile your training session plans for your hypnotherapy practitioner course and your continuing professional development courses utilizing the template shown below for guidance.

	TRAINING SESSION PLAN	
		Duration
TRAINING SESSION OBJECTIVES		
TEACHING ACTIVITY	**LEARNING ACTIVITY**	**TIMING**

LEARNING PRINCIPLES

Learning Psychology

Learning psychology principles

Educational psychology has outlined a number of learning principles and learning theories which spell out the ways in which your trainee can optimize his learning potential as an instinctive human trait.

Your tutorial function will be not only to organize and to manage the learning environment but also to select and to devise teaching activity for your trainee in order to maximize his learning potential. There will be a number of factors for you to observe when conducting your training courses with particular reference to your individual training sessions and your live interaction with your learners in terms of training delivery principles and learning activity.

Training delivery

If possible a single training session should consist of an introductory phase, a developmental phase and a conclusive phase. You will, by this means, be adopting the policy of telling your trainee what he is about to learn, teaching him and then reminding him of what he has learned.

You should, in general, aim to link new learning material to previously acquired knowledge and skill in order to consolidate what you have already imparted and what your trainee has previously assimilated in order to build on his established foundation.

When devising teaching activity for your adult learner it will always be essential for you to focus on his ultimate requirements. By adopting this stance you will be able to maintain an awareness of your trainee's training needs, his abilities and his energy-levels rather than simply working in a vacuum.

Training activity

Acquiring both knowledge and skill will demand experiential learning and participative involvement in the learning process on the part of your trainee.

The most effective teaching will actively Involve your trainee in his own learning process as trainee-centred learning (also known as *Andragogic Learning*). Engage your learner, consequently, as much as possible in his own learning process rather than merely presenting information dryly to him while he becomes a passive recipient. You will, of course, need to strive for a judicious balance between an active learning experience and a passive learning experience for your trainee.

You can maintain your trainee's interest by frequently varying the type of activity which he will undertake as much as possible in order to ensure that he will be continually motivated and, thereby, interested in his own learning experience.

Changing tack regularly, consequently, will mean that the attention-span of your trainee will not be over-stretched. You should similarly make your trainee's learning activity relevant and meaningful.

You can also ensure that the energy-level of your trainee does not flag by breaking down large chunks of the learning into small steps. When presenting fresh information, therefore, you should ensure that it can be delivered in bite-size chunks rather than as an unwieldy whole.

When working with your training group you should, furthermore, foster interactive learning whereby your course-participants can learn from each other. You should, for this reason, utilize plentiful practical activity.

LEARNING PSYCHOLOGY ASSIGNMENT

Answer the questions shown below about learning psychology, pose any further questions which might arise during this process and decide what action, if any, you propose to take as a result of your findings.

- Does your training course programme conform to a logical structure?
- Does your training session structure have a beginning, a middle and an ending?
- Can you introduce new material to your training group together with a reminder of what has gone before during your training programme?
- Do your training sessions incorporate a blend of both theoretical information learning and practical skill activity learning?
- Will your trainee be provided with ample opportunity to practice his skill in order to ensure that he can acquire fluency and apply intuition in the delivery of therapeutic techniques?
- Does your trainee undertake practical activity effortlessly and with confidence?
- Does your trainee wholeheartedly engage with his own learning process?

- Has your trainee become an active participant in terms of the way in which he acquires theoretical knowledge and applies practical skill?

- Are you able to maintain the interest of your trainee by frequently changing the learning activity in which he engages?

- Do your trainees have plentiful opportunity to learn from each other?

Process-Based Educational Theory

Process-based theory principles

Process-based educational theory will consider the route by which your trainee might acquire knowledge and skill within the training context. Process-based theory, therefore, will examine training activity and teaching methodology in order to ensure that your trainee can be given the optimum chance of learning success.

An appreciation of process-based theory will empower you to exploit every opportunity for utilizing effective teaching methodology in order to maximize the learning potential of your trainee.

Knowledge acquisition

An appreciation of the principles of knowledge acquisition in which your trainee will engage should be of great assistance to you in selecting teaching methodology.

Your trainee will at some stage during his learning experience be required to acquire some facts usually as supportive material for his practical work. When acquiring knowledge, therefore, your trainee may be requested to listen, watch, read, note and memorize information.

Knowledge acquisition should challenge your trainee so that he can gain insight and understanding in order to be able to accomplish any given task successfully, accurately and confidently. Your trainee, consequently, will need to absorb information and to commit facts to memory. This information must then be retrieved from your trainee's memory so that he can apply the knowledge which he has acquired in order to accommodate his specific needs.

Knowledge acquisition will be effective for your trainee if the data to be imparted can be structured and presented by you in an easily understandable format. Your trainee should thus be able to easily comprehend what he is learning and to understand conceptually what you are imparting so that he can readily assimilate his knowledge.

Knowledge should, furthermore, be imparted to your trainee in meaningful bite-sized chunks and built up gradually in component steps moving from the known to the unknown. You might, for instance, elect to reinforce and to recapitulate what your trainee might be learning and to back up what you say with a visual representation of the information to be acquired. You will also need to tune into your trainee's learning ability and to pace your training activity accordingly.

When you ask your trainee to acquire his knowledge you will probably utilize presentation, demonstration, discussion, questioning and project-work teaching methodology.

SKILL ACQUISITION

An appreciation of the principles of skill acquisition in which your trainee will engage should be of great assistance to you in selecting teaching methodology (see Figure 14: *SKILL ACQUISITION*).

When acquiring skill your trainee may be asked to observe, to practice and to imitate the performance techniques of others. Skill acquisition should challenge your trainee so that he can accomplish any given task successfully, accurately and confidently.

The Dreyfus model of skill acquisition, devised by the researchers Stuart Dreyfus and Hubert Dreyfus, claims that your learner will undergo a process in order to develop his problem-solving faculties during a skilled performance. The Dreyfus model states that your learner would normally progress from being a novice who improves, becomes proficient, gains expertise and finally acquires mastery over the performance of his skill.

During the skill-development process your learner should gradually become able to recollect, to recognize and to analyse information in order to perfect his decision-making ability and his overall awareness during the performance of his skill. Your learner's progress will gradually be built up with continued practice and he will assume a transition from strict rigidity to unconscious fluidity.

Even though the Dreyfus model of skill acquisition delineated five distinctive stages it should be emphasized that each phase will meld into the next until your learner has acquired his skill and he can relax totally during its performance. The Dreyfus model can be applied not only to a psychomotor skill but also to a mental performance skill such as hypnotherapy practice.

When acquiring skill your trainee should be in a position to experiment with and to explore his own way of working as a means of extending his level of practical competence. When conducting a hypnotherapy session, for instance, your trainee should aim to exhibit a high degree of fluency, automaticity and effortlessness in the performance of his task.

When you ask your trainee to acquire his skill you will probably utilize demonstration, discussion, questioning, supervised practice and project-work teaching methodology.

Figure 14: Skill Acquisition

Skill Level	Learning Activity
Novice	Trainee adheres rigidly to rules and makes no independent decisions
Competence	Trainee perceives component actions and applies his planned routine
Proficiency	Trainee deviates from his planned routine and becomes adaptable in decision-making
Expertise	Trainee relies less on rules and grasps the whole intuitively
Mastery	Trainee perceives possibilities, adopts an analytical approach to new situations, maintains unconscious fluidity, exhibits automaticity and demonstrates an intuitive approach

Active learning

Active learning will occur when your trainee has been requested to engage in practical activity (see Figure 15: *Active Learning*).

An active learning experience should form a major part of your hypnotherapy teaching because your trainee should actively engage in his own learning process. Your trainee will be undertaking active learning, for instance, during practice sessions while you become passive as the overseer of such activity. Your trainee, on the other hand, will become relatively passive while you are imparting knowledge and when you are taking an active role in the teaching arena.

Practical learning activity for your trainee may usually take the form of a hypnotherapy technique practice, a homework research assignment or a problem-solving discussion session for your training group.

Obviously the more active your trainee can be during his learning experience then the more he will learn but, of course, you should not overtire him with too much activity because this ploy will be counter-productive.

It will usually, of course, be more appropriate for your trainee as an adult learner to focus on active learning as he will have extensive experience of the world and, indeed, the learning process – however scanty his formal education might be.

If you take an over-active role, on the other hand, while your trainee might be relatively passive he may zone out and not acquire the skill and knowledge which he seeks.

The level of your trainee's active learning can be measured on a continuum as a basic rule of thumb. Active learning, for instance, can vary from a mere recognition and recall of facts at the lower end of the scale towards a fully autonomous level of ability geared towards active decision-making and the process of making value-judgements at the top end of the spectrum.

FIGURE 15: ACTIVE LEARNING

LEARNING LEVEL	LEARNING ACTIVITY
Low	Trainee recognizes and recalls information
Moderately low	Trainee comprehends and interprets information
Medium low	Trainee applies learned principles
Medium high	Trainee analyses component parts of the whole
Moderately high	Trainee combines and synthesizes elements
High	Trainee takes decisions and makes value-judgements

PASSIVE LEARNING

Passive learning will occur when your trainee adopts a receptive role during his learning experience (see Figure 16: *PASSIVE LEARNING*).

A passive learning experience on the part of your trainee will occur when he becomes the recipient of the information which you are imparting. Passive learning activity may take the form of quietly listening to your theory exposition, the observation of a hypnotherapy technique demonstration or an opportunity to witness a fellow-trainee giving a talk.

There will be occasions when your trainee will need to be engaged in passive learning as his means of acquiring knowledge and working towards acquiring skill. A passive learning activity can, therefore, be just as useful as an active learning experience for your trainee because he will need to have the subject-matter explained and he must be given a chance to have his questions answered by his tutorial guide.

The level of your trainee's passive learning can be measured on a continuum as a basic rule of thumb. Passive learning, for instance, can vary from merely receiving stimuli at one end of the scale to internalizing values which have been imposed on him at the higher end of the spectrum.

FIGURE 16: PASSIVE LEARNING

Learning Level	Learning Activity
Low	Trainee receives external stimuli
Moderately low	Trainee responds to expectations
Medium	Trainee alters beliefs and convictions
Moderately high	Trainee exhibits appropriate behaviour
High	Trainee characterizes internalized values

Process-Based Theory Assignment

Answer the questions shown below about process-based educational theory, pose any further questions which might arise during this process and decide what action, if any, you propose to take as a result of your findings.

- Do you understand what the most effective learning route might be for your trainee?
- Do you appreciate the way in which your trainee can most effectively acquire knowledge?
- Can you arrange your teaching activity so that you are imparting knowledge in small steps with secure links between each?
- Can you enhance your teaching activity by including summary, repetition and visual representation of the information which you intend to impart?
- Do you appreciate the importance of the skill component in hypnotherapy practitioner training?
- What are the various component stages of acquiring a practical skill?
- Can you observe the progress which your trainee will be making in acquiring a usable skill?

- In what proportions do you utilize active learning and passive learning with your trainee?

- In what circumstances might you employ passive learning techniques with your trainee?

- Can you appreciate the need to strike a healthy balance between active learning and passive learning methodology with your trainee?

Learning-Based Educational Theory

Learning-Based Theory Principles

Learning-based educational theory will consider the way in which your trainee might personally acquire knowledge and skill within the training context (see Figure 17: *Learning-Based Educational Theory*).

Learning-based educational theory will focus on the way in which your trainee might acquire learning and the way in which change will occur from a psychological standpoint. Learning-based theory will also consider the instinctive drives which will urge your trainee to acquire knowledge and skill in the interests of human survival.

Part of the survival of the human species will be entwined within the human psyche as a need to acquire knowledge and skill in order to survive. Mankind must conquer his environment in order to ensure his own survival and the survival of the human species. Your trainee, consequently, will need to adapt in order to survive in the world in which he resides with others. Your trainee, for instance, will be required to conquer the unknown in order to become the master of his immediate environment. Once you can appreciate the survivalist drive which your trainee will possess you will not be mystified or uncertain about why he will strive for success during his learning experience.

An appreciation of learning-based theory will allow you to consider the most effective way in which your trainee will organize his own learning experience.

FIGURE 17: LEARNING-BASED EDUCATIONAL THEORY

LEARNING THEORY	LEARNING CHARACTERISTICS
Behavioural	Trainee undertakes habit-forming activity
Cognitive	Trainee undergoes mental changes
Affective	Trainee reacts psychologically
Self-awareness	Trainee seeks to improve his self-image
Humanistic	Trainee desires to make discoveries
Gestalt	Trainee grasps whole meanings
Experiential	Trainee draws on his personal experience

Behavioural learning

The theory of behavioural learning focuses on observing the habit-forming activity of your trainee with regard to acquiring learning.

Your trainee's acquisition of knowledge and skill, consequently, will result in behavioural changes which will indicate that he has reached his learning goal. Your learner may, consequently, acquire learning from a behavioural modification standpoint. This type of learner will usually wish to reshape his behaviour in some way so that his actions can become instinctive.

You might wish to encourage your learner, however, not to attempt to learn everything by rote and repetition as he might have been asked to do while at school. Your trainee may, for instance, rely heavily on his own memory and his intellect in a rather pedestrian fashion. You might, alternatively, seek to encourage your learner to be more flexible in the way in which he unconsciously absorbs information, he gains insight and he utilizes knowledge and skill as your means of preparing him for working practice.

Cognitive learning

The theory of cognitive learning considers the way in which your learner's mind will acquire knowledge and skill and the mental processes which he will undergo in order to attain his learning goal.

You will need to evaluate your learner's mental changes by way of assessing whether his learning goal has been achieved. Your trainee, for instance, will need to develop his memory, to gain understanding and to fully comprehend the subject-matter being studied.

Your trainee should also apply the skill and knowledge which he has acquired and then evaluate his own performance in order to demonstrate adequate learning in practice. Your trainee should ideally aim to apply principles and to make generalisations about the subject-matter being studied in order to gauge the effectiveness of his learning experience. Your trainee, moreover, will need to augment his existing knowledge and skill in order to add to his repertoire of experiences during the learning process.

Affective learning

The theory of affective learning evaluates the emotive and the psychological reactions which your trainee will exhibit during his learning experience.

You can usually observe that learning has taken place by noting the level of your trainee's insight into the topic being studied. Your trainee, for instance, may adopt a fresh attitude and will gain deeper insight into a given topic when his perspective has been altered.

Your trainee will, ultimately, observe a situation and he will accordingly make value-judgements about the subject-matter which he has absorbed. Your trainee, therefore, will alter his belief systems and his personal-value systems once his learning goal has been attained. Your trainee, for instance, must appreciate the importance of his future role as a working professional who will be responsible for helping his clients in an ethical manner.

Self-awareness learning

The theory of self-awareness learning (also known as *Personality-Oriented Learning*) adumbrates that your trainee will acquire learning most effectively when he believes that his performance will improve his self-image and his self-concept.

A competitive learner will strive for mastery over his subject-matter as if in the race for human survival. You should, therefore, be able to observe when your trainee might be acutely aware of his effect on others and then assess whether he will strive accordingly to master his learning aim in a spirit of competition.

If your trainee is very aware of his effect and his influence on others then he may constantly consider his own self-image in the presence of his fellow-trainees. This type of learner, however, may become overly concerned with his personal achievements during his learning experience and he may constantly be gauging his progress against that of his colleagues.

Your trainee with an over-developed sense of self-awareness, therefore, may be super-sensitive if he considers himself to be performing poorly as opposed to being stimulated by the challenge of competing with others. You should, of course, endeavour to temper the over-reactiveness of such a trainee in order to equip him for working practice so that he will not be continually judging himself and reacting adversely in consequence.

Humanistic learning

The theory of humanistic learning believes that your trainee will have an enquiring mind and that he will have a need to discover new territory for himself.

As part of the human survivalist instinct your trainee will have a desire to explore, to experiment and to investigate the world about him. You should be able to observe, consequently, that your trainee will have a basic need to be self-directed and this trait, in itself, will fuel his motivation and will enhance his self-concept.

Gestalt learning

The theory of gestalt learning maintains that your trainee may have a propensity to take an overview of the topic to be mastered and that he will, consequently, acquire learning as a whole entity rather than as a series of component parts.

Your trainee thus will have an inherent power to gain insight and he will unconsciously seek this lofty ideal when acquiring his knowledge and skill.

You should, therefore, observe your trainee's tendency to conceptualize and to perceive his subject-matter as a complete entity and, in so doing, he can gain profound insight and understanding about his study.

Experiential learning

The theory of experiential learning states that your trainee will have a need to learn by drawing on his own personal experience and his inherent interests.

Your trainee's learning experience will thus be influenced by his concrete past experience combined with his ability to conceive and to apply concepts during his learning process. You should, consequently, be able to observe your trainee's desire to be intellectually stimulated and to be responsive to new and interesting subject-matter which might relate to his past experience.

You will also, of course, need to appreciate the previous experience of your learner in order to understand his particular experiential learning mechanism.

LEARNING-BASED THEORY ASSIGNMENT

Answer the questions shown below about learning-based educational theory, pose any further questions which might arise during this process and decide what action, if any, you propose to take as a result of your findings.

- Can you appreciate the benefit of understanding learning-based educational psychology theory?

- Have you noted any changes in the habits and the behaviours of your trainee which would signify that learning has taken place?

- Does your trainee rely solely on rote-learning and his memory faculty in order to acquire knowledge and skill?

- Can you identify any ways in which your trainee has acquired comprehension of the subject-matter?

- Can you detect any ways in which your trainee has gained insight or changed his attitude towards the topic which he might be studying?

- Do you find that your trainee can learn more effectively in a group setting?

- Do you consider that your trainee will be overly-concerned with the impression which he might create in the eyes of others?

- Can you observe the ways in which your trainee will wish to better himself by acquiring knowledge and skill?

- Does your trainee perceive meaningful wholes when studying a given topic or does he tend to rely purely on his memory?

- Does your trainee learn more effectively when he can draw on his past experience of learning?

Context-Based Educational Theory

Context-based theory principles

Context-based educational theory will consider the environment in which your trainee might acquire knowledge and skill within the training context (see Figure 18: *Context-Based Educational Theory*).

Context-based educational theory will focus on the situation in which your trainee will acquire learning so that his environment can be rendered optimally conducive to his learning goal.

You will, consequently, need to organize the learning environment in order to ensure that it will be most suitable to your trainee's learning experience.

An appreciation of context-based theory will enable you to arrange the training habitat and to organize the teaching resources for your trainee's highest benefit.

FIGURE 18: CONTEXT-BASED EDUCATIONAL THEORY

LEARNING THEORY	LEARNING CHARACTERISTICS
Human communication	Trainee possesses an inherent instinct to communicate with others
Social interaction	Trainee possesses an inherent instinct to interact with others
Environmental engagement	Trainee becomes driven to engage with his surroundings
Situational activity	Trainee desires stimulating experience
Critical appraisal	Trainee becomes motivated by challenge
Critical reflection	Trainee requires problem-solving activity
Diversity	Trainee craves varied activity
Constructivist interaction	Trainee seeks a knowledgeable teacher

Human-communication learning

The theory of human-communication learning states that the human organism will possess an inherent need to reach out to others in the social habitat in which he resides in order to conquer his environment in his struggle for survival.

Your trainee, for instance, will have an inherent desire to communicate with others in the world about him and to acquire learning in order to maintain his position in a society devoid of chaos. Your trainee might also retain an inherent desire to feel that he has fulfilled an important mission in life, that he has optimized his human potential and that he has made a contribution to society.

Social-interaction learning

The theory of social-interaction learning maintains that the human animal will have an instinctive need to interact with others in the society in which he dwells. Social-interaction learning theory sees your trainee as a pack animal whose survival will be reliant on his ability to socialize with others. The theory of social-interaction learning states, therefore, that your trainee may be best motivated to learn in a social context.

Your trainee can usefully make contact with fellow-learners, exchange his ideas with others and share his experiences in a spirit of co-operative participation. You should hence be able to observe that your trainee will have an inherent need to actively engage with and to interact with others from whom he can learn in a fertile environment.

Your trainee will undoubtedly wish to better himself and to be seen to have done so in the eyes of his peers. This hypothesis hence will render the group-training experience one in which your trainee will feel a sense of camaraderie provided that he does not feel at all threatened by the group environment.

If your trainee is strongly aware of those about him and he can relate well to others then he may actually learn more effectively through social interaction. If your learner responds to social interaction you could easily aim to provide plentiful opportunity for him to engage with others. Practice sessions and group discussion will typically cater for your trainee's need to be gregarious.

When your learner relishes social interaction he may not, however, warm to home-study since it will lack the social stimulation which he instinctively craves.

ENVIRONMENTAL-ENGAGEMENT LEARNING

The theory of environmental-engagement learning purports that your trainee will possess an instinctive drive to relate to his social and his cultural sphere and to engage with his immediate environment in order to gain mastery over his habitat.

Your trainee does not exist in the world in isolation from the culture and the society of which he is a part. Your trainee thus will wish to qualify and to survive professionally in the cut-and-thrust of the world of work. Your trainee will, therefore, adhere to the unwritten laws of society in which each individual must take on the responsibility of developing himself to the best of his ability.

SITUATIONAL-ACTIVITY LEARNING

The theory of situational-activity learning views your trainee as having a requirement to engage in an activity which can stimulate him and can maintain his interest.

If your trainee's interest can be fully maintained then learning will be the natural result of his thirst for education. Your role will thus be to ensure that your trainee can be sufficiently well motivated and that the subject-matter will be fascinating, relevant and alluring.

CRITICAL-APPRAISAL LEARNING

The theory of critical-appraisal learning (also known as *Information Processing Learning*) adumbrates that your trainee will need to be motivated by a challenge and that he will wish to compete with others in the race for human survival.

Your trainee, consequently, will need to be stretched so that he can achieve his learning objective and hence he can feel the satisfaction of having accomplished something of value in the social world.

If your trainee tends to learn by efficiently processing the facts which you impart then he will undoubtedly be equipped to learn from an academic standpoint because he will readily handle facts intellectually. Your trainee may, consequently, be able to comprehend complex theories, to organize varying concepts and to solve problems effortlessly.

When your trainee approaches his subject-matter from an academic standpoint he will have no difficulty in juggling complexities. Your trainee who works in this way should, of course, reinforce his learning experience with practical work so that the dry theoretical content of his learning can be applied in live working practice.

CRITICAL-REFLECTION LEARNING

The theory of critical-reflection learning upholds that your trainee will have an intellectual need to undertake stimulating problem-solving activity. The human race is a species with intellect which sets mankind above other animals in order to come to terms with the environment.

Your trainee, therefore, will be inclined to search for knowledge and he will be selective when sifting and sorting information. Your trainee will also be equipped to analyse, to conceptualize and to make discoveries for himself.

Once knowledge and skill has been acquired your trainee will then display a need to make meaningful and purposeful decisions about his future.

Diversity learning

The theory of diversity learning claims that your trainee will learn best when his learning activity can be varied and he can easily move between active learning activity and passive learning activity in order to optimize his chances of success.

You should, therefore, ensure that your trainee can be given plentiful opportunity for experiencing varied training activity in order to ensure that he can tackle the subject-matter from a number of different angles.

Adequate variety can usually, of course, be attained with a healthy blend of active learning and passive learning methodology.

Constructivist-interaction learning

The theory of constructivist-interaction learning advocates that your trainee will require a teacher in order to bridge the gap between his lack of knowledge and skill and its acquisition.

When your trainee acquires a teacher he will be taking the shortest possible route away from ignorance towards enlightenment with the aid of a knowledgeable person.

As a teacher you can, therefore, assist your trainee to assimilate learning by incorporating new experiences into his existing knowledge and by dovetailing his new learning into his view of the world.

GROUP LEARNING

Group learning will have the positive advantage of providing an opportunity for your trainee to share and to air his ideas in a supportive learning environment as a means of enhancing the learning experience for each member of your training group.

The group environment will afford much opportunity for context-based educational theories to be fulfilled by your trainee.

The group environment will generally allow your trainee to reinforce his learning, will spur him on to learn more and will endorse his learning process by gaining feedback from others.

Often the group-dynamic will become both a challenge and a reward for your trainee who participants fully with like-minded people. Your trainee may suffer, however, if the group-dynamic is not conducive to his learning experience – particularly if there might be an imbalance of learning ability and personality traits within your training group.

If one trainee, for instance, seeks to dominate your training group then other less assertive personalities may feel inhibited as a result. Your role, in the circumstances, will be to temper the excessive enthusiasm of some trainees while simultaneously ensuring that you draw out and include the more reticent in your training group during the learning process.

INDIVIDUAL LEARNING

Individual learning may be undertaken for your trainee who might need some special assistance or some private coaching on a one-to-one basis.

One-to-one tuition can assist your trainee who may be threatened by a hostile group-dynamic, for instance, when special attention and nurturing will be most appropriate for him.

CONTEXT-BASED THEORY ASSIGNMENT

Answer the questions shown below about context-based educational theory, pose any further questions which might arise during this process and decide what action, if any, you propose to take as a result of your findings.

- Can you appreciate the fact that your trainee will be propelled by a number of unconscious and instinctive drives when he undergoes his learning experience?

- Can you see the way in which your trainee will be driven by a need to communicate, to interact and to socialize with others during his learning experience?

- Do you appreciate the way in which your trainee will engage with his social and his cultural environment as part of his thirst for education?

- Can you identify the way in which your trainee might learn by a desire for the critical appraisal of information?

- Are you aware of the way in which your trainee might reflect on his newly acquired knowledge and skill?

- Have you observed that the critical appraisal of facts and intellectual reflection are a feature of the human condition?

- Are you fully appreciative of the necessity and the importance of your role as a tutor for your trainee?
- Does your training group exhibit a healthy group-dynamic?
- Might there be an occasion when you will need to intervene with the development of a group-dynamic?
- Might your trainee warrant some individual tuition on occasion?

LEARNING STRATEGY

LEARNING STRATEGY PRINCIPLES

A learning strategy will constitute the way in which your trainee will approach his learning experience and, in consequence, how he can incorporate the subject-matter into his personal information processing system (see Figure 19: *LEARNING STRATEGY*).

A learning strategy will dictate the way in which your trainee will unconsciously respond to his learning experience and how he can adopt an individualistic learning style for acquiring knowledge and skill. Your trainee, consequently, will find an optimal way in which he can maximize his learning experience. You will need, therefore, to detect the way in which your trainee will engage in all learning activity in order to capitalize on his inherent talent and his unique inclinations.

An appreciation of the principal learning strategy which your trainee may adopt will hence enable you to become a more effective tutor. Your trainee may think and act in various ways which will be indicative of his unconscious learning strategy. You should easily be able to identify your trainee's way of acquiring both knowledge and skill after some careful observation.

FIGURE 19: LEARNING STRATEGY

LEARNING STYLE	LEARNING CHARACTERISTICS
Active engagement	Trainee actively engages with the subject-matter
Reflective	Trainee undertakes thoughtful contemplation about the subject-matter
Theoretical	Trainee formulates a theory about the subject-matter
Experiential	Trainee experiments with the subject-matter
Analogical	Trainee relates his known experience to the unknown subject-matter
Perceptive	Trainee perceives the subject-matter as a whole
Imitative practice	Trainee learns the subject-matter by imitating the practice of others

ACTIVE-ENGAGEMENT LEARNING

An active-engagement learning strategy will become evident when your trainee remains active and industrious and he fully engages with the subject-matter during his learning experience.

If your trainee tends to adopt an active-engagement learning style he will have a need for direct experience when undertaking any learning activity. You should, therefore, ensure that your trainee can actively participate in practical tasks which will instil and reinforce his learning experience.

Your trainee will require some form of physical activity or practical action in order to achieve a high skill component during his learning process. A practice session, for instance, would empower your trainee to learn by putting into live practice what he might have learned theoretically about a given therapeutic technique.

REFLECTIVE LEARNING

A reflective learning strategy will become evident when your trainee can carefully mull over the content of the subject-matter during his learning experience.

Your trainee may learn most effectively by undergoing a process of thoughtful reflection. If your trainee adopts a reflective learning route he will have a need to observe and to make value-judgements about the knowledge and the skill which he may be acquiring.

Your teaching approach can encourage your trainee to consider, to discuss, to contemplate and to evaluate at length the subject-matter which you are imparting. Your role will thus be to guide your trainee so that he can consolidate his learning by interpreting facts and then developing concepts about his learning topic. Your trainee could be requested to conduct a practice session, for instance, and then be invited to reflect in detail on his practical experience.

Theoretical learning

A theoretical learning strategy will become evident when your trainee can formulate a theory about the content of his learning experience.

Your trainee may wish to question and to consider his learning topic in order to draw some form of conclusion from which his theory can transpire. Your trainee will need to formulate his own guidelines, therefore, during his learning experience so that he will have a working frame of reference.

You can tailor your training activity in order to include a formula or a blueprint for working practice outcomes so that you can provide a theoretical angle for your trainee. Your trainee could be invited, for instance, to formulate a set of guidelines about how to construct a client-session and then make some value-judgements accordingly.

Experimental learning

An experimental learning strategy will become evident when your trainee can undertake some form of experimentation during his learning experience.

Your trainee may wish to experiment repeatedly with the subject-matter which you are conveying to him. Typically your trainee will have a need not only to formulate a theory but also to test out his hypotheses in a reality-setting.

Your training approach might typically embrace a means of asking your trainee to conduct a series of experiments in order to observe and to note the results. Your trainee could, for example, formulate a series of plans for utilizing a given therapeutic technique and then be invited to experiment with and to test his theories in practice in order to ascertain which works best for him in any given set of circumstances.

ANALOGICAL LEARNING

An analogical learning strategy will become evident when your trainee can immediately relate any new subject-matter to his previous learning experience. Your trainee may, therefore, process information by constantly drawing an analogy between what he might currently be studying and the learning which he has acquired previously.

Your learner, for instance, may draw on his existing knowledge and experience in order to compare like with like during the process of introducing fresh matter into his mind. During this process your trainee will be drawing information from one source in order to assist with problem-solving and reasoning in another. Your trainee, by this means, will be utilizing the essence of any existing learning and then applying his previous understanding in similar circumstances.

You can assist your trainee by frequently drawing comparisons, securing links and making reference to material which he has previously studied.

Perceptive learning

A perceptive learning strategy will become evident when your trainee can perceive any new topic as an entire entity during his learning experience. Your trainee may, therefore, acquire learning by perceiving an entire structure as a single entity rather than having to break down the whole into discrete units of information.

When your trainee can perceive the whole picture he will be able to construct patterns from the key ingredients of a complex whole. If your trainee, for instance, learns to conduct a given therapeutic technique by noting the various sections and the junction-points of a single unit he will then perceive the whole and the way in which its component parts are interconnected.

Imitative-practice learning

An imitative-practice learning strategy will become evident when your trainee can copy the actions of another during his learning experience. Your learner may, therefore, acquire a new skill by watching a demonstration or seeing an example and then putting his freshly acquired knowledge into practice.

When acquiring a new skill in order to learn a given therapeutic technique, for instance, your trainee may wish to observe a live demonstration of a therapeutic practice technique and then be given an opportunity for personal practice. Often this route will be the most sensible one for imparting such learning to your hypnotherapy trainees.

LEARNING STRATEGY ASSIGNMENT

Answer the questions shown below about learning strategy, pose any further questions which might arise during this process and decide what action, if any, you propose to take as a result of your findings.

- Do you fully understand the learning strategy which your trainee will adopt in order to acquire his knowledge and skill?
- Is your trainee more than eager to learn by an active participation in his learning experience?
- Is your trainee prone to reflection and contemplation as his means of effectively acquiring his knowledge and skill?

- Might your trainee need to formulate a theory which he can then set about proving to himself as his means of optimizing his learning experience?

- Can your trainee gain insight from his practical learning experience?

- Can you detect the way in which your trainee might relate new material to his previously acquired knowledge and skill?

- Can you find a means of enhancing your trainee's learning experience by linking his past experience of hypnotherapy to his present learning activity?

- Would your trainee be able to practice a new therapeutic technique from a brief outline rather than from a practical demonstration of that technique?

- Can you encourage your trainee to view the whole picture as well as any specific detail?

- Does your trainee benefit from witnessing the practice methodology of others prior to conducting a given therapeutic session?

LEARNER MOTIVATION

LEARNER MOTIVATION PRINCIPLES

You should aim to acquire the art of learner motivation in order to teach your trainee most effectively. Your trainee essentially can be motivated to learn successfully provided that you can observe a number of key factors when designing your teaching programme.

You will need to empower your learner to become self-directed so that he can tap into his own intrinsic ability to acquire knowledge and skill as an instinctive and survivalist human capacity.

Your trainee, consequently, will need a reason for his learning which he can easily identify. Your learner, moreover, should be able to see the relevance of the subject-matter which you are imparting and the significance of the learning activity which you will subsequently ask him to undertake. Your trainee should, therefore, discover the way in which his own learning process will be unfolding and unravelling.

You will not normally encounter undue worry about motivating your adult trainees but you should identify the motivational needs of each learner in order to maximize the effectiveness of your teaching activity.

Your adult learner's motivation may stem from a number of different sources and your task will simply be to identify and to capitalize on this wellspring in order to fully exploit his motivational drive.

Intrinsic motivation

Your trainee's motivation may spring from an intrinsic source whereby he will be interested in the subject-matter being imparted – virtually for its own sake – and he will then gain the consequent personal satisfaction from his own learning experience.

Your trainee obviously will need to appreciate the value of what he is learning in order to become self-motivated so that he can discover, explore and apply the knowledge and the skill which he will be endeavouring to acquire.

You should be able to detect whether your trainee has an intrinsic interest in the topic which you are presenting and you should decipher whether any particular theme might be of special interest as a motivational force.

Aspirational motivation

Your trainee's motivation may arise from his personal career aspirations because this form of motivation will inherently incorporate a future consequential value.

You might be advised to gauge the career aspirations of your trainee, consequently, in order to ensure that you can tailor your training activity towards his individualistic goal.

Your learner should be motivated so that he can cope in any real-life situation. Your trainee will probably wish to take up self-employment and to survive in the competitive world of work – albeit that some trainees may elect not to start up in practice after your course has concluded.

Your trainee will also need to draw on his previous knowledge and skills – perhaps from a myriad of life-experiences – in order to maximize his learning potential when aspiring to achieve his learning goal.

Social motivation

Your trainee's motivation may arise from a social standpoint whereby he will seek praise from others as a result of his acquired learning.

In the struggle for human survival your trainee may also gain the satisfaction of knowing that he has exceeded his own learning expectations when comparing himself with others.

You can often measure the degree to which your trainee will feel proud of what he might have achieved by taking the route towards qualifying as a practitioner or by furthering his career in the professional world.

You will also need to consider any of your learner's unhelpful external and internal pressures which may be created in the social environment. You might be advised, for instance, not to encourage a competitive atmosphere in your training group as this may diminish the self-confidence of your trainee who might suffer as a result of the personal challenge of competition in the training environment.

LEARNER MOTIVATION ASSIGNMENT

Answer the questions shown below about learner motivation, pose any further questions which might arise during this process and decide what action, if any, you propose to take as a result of your findings.

- Are you able to ensure that your trainee will be continually stimulated throughout his training programme so that he can acquire the appropriate knowledge and skill?
- Can your trainee continually see the relevance of the subject-matter which you are imparting and the way in which his learning journey will be unfolding?

- Have you clearly identified the motivational needs of each of your trainees?
- Does your trainee possess an intrinsic motivation which will bring him untold reward?
- Does your trainee have a special interest in a given topic which you could exploit to the full for his own benefit during his learning voyage?
- Will your trainee have become fully competent in terms of your course objectives by the end of his training period?
- Does your trainee have any unrealistic expectations of himself?
- Does your trainee continually seek praise from others and then judge himself adversely as a result?
- Does your trainee constantly debase his own achievements?
- Will your trainee have optimized his learning potential by the end of his learning experience with you?

Learner Nurturing

Learner nurturing principles

You will be working in a caring capacity when tutoring your trainee because he will need to be nurtured, supported, encouraged and developed during his learning process.

You should, consequently, foster and draw out of your trainee his learning potential so that he can achieve his personal best and can become fulfilled by his learning experience. You must also be a sturdy support for your trainee when he encounters emotive turmoil during his learning experience.

Trainee rapport

You will need to foster and to maintain an efficacious rapport with your trainee which can guide him speedily, effectively and safely along his learning path.

You should, consequently, understand, respect and consider your trainee throughout his course in order to maintain rapport.

You ought to treat your adult learner as an equal at all times even though you have become his guide and his mentor. Your respectful stance will safely steer your trainee through his learning experience and will ultimately enable him to put his learning into viable working practice.

TRAINEE CHAMPIONING

You should ensure that your trainee can appreciate that you are his champion as well as his guide and his mentor. Your trainee should be left in no doubt at all about the fact that you are approachable and that you will always be there to assist him.

Your general policy might be to continually praise your trainee's efforts in order to motivate him and to stimulate his further interest. You can, by this means, convey to your trainee that he can acquire knowledge and skill in a safe and non-judgemental context.

Should you need to adversely criticize your trainee in any way then this task should be undertaken gently, discreetly and privately. Adverse criticism of your trainee should, of course, be kept to an absolute minimum in order ensure that he does not become significantly discouraged or irretrievably demotivated.

TRAINEE CHALLENGING

Your trainee will need to be stretched in some way during his learning experience because he will have to rise to the challenge of learning.

The learning challenge, however, should not be a painful experience for your trainee if you are able to steer him skilfully in order to maximize his learning potential. You can assist your trainee, for instance, by offering him a series of realistic and achievable challenges rather than by asking him to climb an impossibly high mountain. A series of bite-sized challenges will promote self-discovery for your trainee which will, in turn, act as a motivational force.

Your trainee should be abundantly aware of his own successful progress throughout your course. When your trainee can clearly identify his own progress this factor will, in itself, stimulate him to further effort and should maintain his perpetual interest.

TRAINEE COLLABORATION

You should continually encourage your trainee's co-operation and collaboration within his training group. Your trainee will learn in a collaborative atmosphere by an exchange of views, a sharing of experiences and a spirit of conducive social interaction.

A highly competitive atmosphere within a group, however, may be an unhealthy and a self-defeating means of motivating your adult learner who may feel threatened by such an environment.

LEARNER NURTURING ASSIGNMENT

Answer the questions shown below about learner nurturing, pose any further questions which might arise during this process and decide what action, if any, you propose to take as a result of your findings.

- Do you fully appreciate your role as a guide and a mentor of your trainee together with your need to provide him with a nurturing learning habitat and a conducive developmental environment?
- Do you understand your trainee sufficiently well to be able to foster and to maintain a healthy rapport with him?
- Can you fully accept your trainee without judgement or personal criticism no matter what his personal limitations?
- Do feel that you can fully support and genuinely champion your trainee?
- Can you provide your trainee with a series of attainable challenges so that he can reach his ultimate learning goal without feeling despondent at any stage of his learning experience?

- Can you provide your trainee with a number of small challenges rather than one insurmountable struggle so that he can feel satisfaction in his achievement throughout his learning experience?
- Can you keep unhealthy competition within your training group to an absolute minimum?
- Can you foster a spirit of co-operation and collaboration between your trainees?
- Do you understand the way in which your trainees will learn from each other when learning experiences are shared?
- Can you gently discourage your trainee from adversely comparing himself with others?

LEARNER ASSESSMENT

LEARNER ASSESSMENT PRINCIPLES

It may be advisable for you to be able to assess the performance of your trainee regularly in order to evaluate his progress and to gauge the effectiveness of your teaching activity.

Any learning assessment should be undertaken primarily for the benefit of your learner who can obtain important feedback about his progress. Your trainee, by this means, can then appreciate how successful he has been in accomplishing his learning task.

During your trainee's learning experience you can assess him either formally or informally as well as continually, periodically or merely at the end of his training course.

The most valuable form of assessment for your adult learner will obviously be self-assessment whereby he can gauge his own progress during his self-directed learning experience.

INFORMAL ASSESSMENT

The informal assessment of your trainee will occur when you obtain casual feedback from him about his progress, his capabilities and his skill acquisition.

Informal assessment will, in most cases, be quite adequate for hypnotherapy training because you will be catering for mature learners who will undoubtedly be able to undertake self-assessment.

Your adult learner will gain his own sense of feedback, for instance, during practice sessions and, therefore, when you oversee your trainee at work this assessment process will be perfectly adequate. When you can observe your trainee in action in this manner you will be able to make an accurate evaluation of his progress and his ability.

Informal assessment can also take the form of questioning your trainee periodically or providing homework assignments during which time he will be free to undertake his own research and to distil his own thoughts.

Informal continuous assessment may be utilized effectively when you regularly monitor your trainee in order to respond appropriately should he fall short of the mark in terms of your course objectives.

Your trainee should, of course, be unaware of the fact that you are observing his performance when you are employing informal assessment methodology.

Formal assessment

The formal assessment of your trainee will take place when you ask him to undertake some form of test or examination from which he will be provided with constructive feedback.

A hypnotherapy course may be constructed to include, for example, a written test or a live practice session as a qualifying assessment for your learner at the end of your training programme.

Assessment methodology evaluation

The value of any form of learner assessment will be necessary so that you can evaluate and, if necessary, you can adjust your teaching methodology accordingly.

If you have observed that your trainee has not grasped a given principle or not understood a specific theory, for example, then some revision may be indicated. Once you have obtained the results of your trainee assessment you can then decide whether information needs to be presented in a different way or whether some recapitulation of former learning might be called for in the circumstances.

When undertaking any form of teaching evaluation, of course, you should remember that your ultimate goal will be to maximize the learning potential of your trainee by providing him with a realistic challenge – yet not demanding that he reach any dizzy heights.

LEARNER ASSESSMENT ASSIGNMENT

Answer the questions shown below about learner assessment, pose any further questions which might arise during this process and decide what action, if any, you propose to take as a result of your findings.

- Do you believe that some form of learner assessment would benefit your trainee?
- Do you consider that by undertaking learner assessment you will personally benefit from the evaluation process?
- Can you devise ways in which you could informally assess the performance of your trainee on each of your training courses?
- Can you closely observe your trainee in order to monitor his progress informally throughout your training programme?
- Can you devise ways in which you could discover the extent to which your trainee has acquired knowledge and skill effectively?
- Does your course include some form of written homework task or project-work assignment?

- Can you include some degree of regular questioning within your training sessions in order to allow your trainee to assess his personal understanding?

- Will your trainee be given an opportunity to assess his own progress throughout your training course?

- Does your course include any manner of formal assessment at the conclusion of your training programme in order to confer a qualifying status on your trainee?

- Do you think that your trainee would adversely react to a formal test which would decide whether he might qualify for practitioner-level status?

Teaching Principles

TEACHING PSYCHOLOGY

TEACHING PSYCHOLOGY PRINCIPLES

Educational psychology has furnished the teaching profession with ways of approaching the task of encouraging your trainee to acquire learning from a global perspective.

Your teaching role will be one of juggling learning objectives, teaching activity, trainee assessment and self-reflection throughout your entire training programme.

Your preparatory task will entail planning your entire course programme, structuring your training sessions, devising training activity, marshalling effective teaching resources and finally evaluating the outcome of your training endeavour.

During your live training delivery you will need to apply teaching principles which are appropriate for adult learners and you should assess the effectiveness of your teaching activity continually.

If you are conversant with the theory of teaching you will thus be able to optimize your trainee's chances of learning success.

THEORETICAL-PRACTICAL TEACHING

Your hypnotherapy training programme should essentially be a judicious mixture of theoretical learning and practical work.

Your trainee will need to appreciate the theoretical background theory on any given topic, the thinking behind a given therapeutic technique and the application of that therapeutic methodology in practice.

When introducing a new therapeutic principle, for instance, you may need to provide a summary of the origin of a given therapeutic methodology, state its inherent principles, demonstrate the way in which it can be undertaken and then allow your trainees adequate time for live therapeutic practice and personal reflection.

When conducting a live therapeutic session, moreover, your trainee should exhibit a high degree of fluency, automaticity and effortlessness in order to be able to practice with confidence and assurance in the workplace.

ACTIVE-PASSIVE TEACHING

You should always ensure that your trainee experiences a workable blend of both active learning activity and passive learning activity when he wishes to acquire knowledge and skill (see Figure 20: *ACTIVE-PASSIVE TEACHING*).

When imparting knowledge, for instance, you may wish to give a series of talks which can generate discussion and questioning so that your trainee will be engaged in both active learning work and passive learning interest.

When encouraging your trainee to develop skill for conducting a hypnotherapy client-session you might, moreover, give a demonstration of a specific technique and then summarize the steps which you have taken. You could next ask your trainee to actively apply the specific principles of the technique in practice while you observe and monitor his performance.

You will, by this means, include within your training programme some passive learning interest for your trainee in the guise of your demonstration combined with a degree of active learning activity by way of discussion and practice. Your trainee could also be asked to report on his learning experience during a given practice session so that your learners can be both actively learning and passively learning from each other. You would also be given an opportunity to informally assess your trainee while he is undertaking his practical assignment and during his practice session feedback.

Figure 20: Active-Passive Teaching

Teaching Activity	Learning Activity	Trainee Activity
Tutor presentation	Trainee gains awareness of therapeutic methodology principles	Passive
Tutor demonstration	Trainee observes and notes therapeutic methodology principles	Active/Passive
Trainee discussion	Trainee discusses therapeutic demonstration	Active/Passive
Trainee questioning	Trainee poses and answers questions about therapeutic demonstration	Active/Passive
Tutor summary	Trainee plans therapeutic practice session	Active/Passive
Trainee practice	Trainee practices therapeutic methodology	Active
Tutor observation	Trainee undergoes informal assessment	Active
Trainee reporting	Trainee reports on practice session	Active
Trainee discussion and questioning	Trainees question and discuss practice session	Active/Passive

TEACHING PSYCHOLOGY ASSIGNMENT

Answer the questions shown below about teaching psychology, pose any further questions which might arise during this process and decide what action, if any, you propose to take as a result of your findings.

- Do you fully appreciate your role as a tutor and why it will be important for you to understand teaching and training psychology?

- Can you review the way in which your course programme has been structured and the way in which each training session has been constructed?

- Can you evaluate the way in which your training activity has been devised and organized?

- In what ways will you plan to assess the effectiveness of your teaching activity with self-reflection?

- By what means will you teach the acquisition of theoretical knowledge and the development of practical skill to your trainee?

- Can you ensure a balance of active learning activity and passive learning pursuit during your training programme in order to enhance your trainee's learning experience?

- How might you utilize an active learning process for your trainee?

- Can you ensure that your trainee participates fully in his own learning experience?

- How might you utilize passive learning activity for your trainee?

- How can you ensure that you do not over-work or over-tire your trainee?

TEACHING STRATEGY

TEACHING STRATEGY PRINCIPLES

You will need to give careful consideration to the way in which you could organize your trainee's learning experience in terms of your teaching strategy (see Figure 21: *TEACHING STRATEGY*).

You should regard yourself as a strategist who will be instrumental in effectively designing the learning process and in organizing the learning environment for your trainee. You should hence design the structure and the delivery of your training programme in the most appropriate way for your trainee.

Your teaching strategy should consider when your trainee will receive his tuition, the way in which his learning will be directed and the means by which you can encourage him to acquire his learning.

FIGURE 21: TEACHING STRATEGY

TEACHING STRATEGY	TEACHING APPLICATION
Episodic teaching	Training programme consists of a number of discrete learning units
Continuous teaching	Training programme consists of one continuous learning unit
Trainee-centred teaching	Teaching activity focuses on the needs of the trainee
Curriculum-oriented teaching	Teaching activity focuses on the trainee's final assessment
Formal teaching	Teaching activity encourages the trainee to adopt a rigid set of rules in his learning approach
Informal teaching	Teaching activity encourages the trainee to be creative and flexible in his learning approach

EPISODIC TEACHING

An episodic training programme structure will constitute a series of short learning units which will be taken at given intervals over an extended period of time normally as a part-time course.

Episodic learning will usually be appropriate for your trainee who wishes to undertake his course as part-time study because he may currently be in a full-time occupation. Episodic learning, therefore, will usually be the most appropriate course structure for a hypnotherapy practitioner training programme. Your trainee may, for instance, attend a number of weekend modules which are undertaken at regular intervals over a period of one or two years.

If your trainee is a working professional who might be undertaking a lengthy continuing professional development programme then an episodic learning structure will permit him to return to his workplace and to put his learning into practice in staggered stages.

Your trainee may be able to assimilate information better over a protracted period of time – especially when he might be required to complete homework assignments which would involve putting his newly acquired learning into practice. When your trainee is in the process of acquiring the relatively complex skill of hypnotherapy practice his mind will also need time to sift and to sort information in order to assimilate his learning effectively.

Continuous teaching

A continuous training programme structure will constitute one complete block of time normally as a full-time course.

Continuous learning will usually be undertaken when the subject-matter can be condensed into a short unit of time so that your trainee will not be required to sacrifice an extended block of time away from his workplace.

A continuous learning course structure may not be appropriate for your practitioner training programme, therefore, but may lend itself ideally to a continuing professional development course because a short course of only a few days or a week will be better tackled as one complete unit.

TRAINEE-CENTRED TEACHING

A trainee-centred teaching strategy will focus on the learning process rather than on your course content and, consequently, your trainee's needs will become the main orientation during his learning experience.

Most hypnotherapy training courses will usually be trainee-centred because your learner will need to be nurtured if he is to become an ethical working professional. Adopting a trainee-centred learning strategy will usually be the most effective means of developing skill in your trainee who can be continually assessed throughout your entire course programme.

With trainee-centred teaching your course programme will be designed as a vocational learning journey – the ultimate aim of which will be for your trainee to set up in professional practice rather than to merely pass a specific qualifying examination.

CURRICULUM-CENTRED TEACHING

A curriculum-centred teaching strategy will focus on a formal assessment examination at the end of your training programme and your trainee will work single-mindedly towards that goal.

While trainee assessment may be an integral part of your hypnotherapy practitioner training this end-view should not become the overarching focus of your attention.

Curriculum-oriented training may also not be the most effective teaching strategy for an adult learner who might feel under pressure to perform well and to produce exemplary results when necessary.

INFORMAL TEACHING

An informal teaching strategy will encourage your trainee to rely on his own personal resources in order to acquire knowledge and skill.

With informal teaching methodology your trainee, consequently, will be able to draw on his own experience, to rely on his own inner resources, to undertake experimentation, to organize his own learning process and to become self-motivated in order to learn. Self-directed learning will, therefore, often be the most appropriate learning strategy for your adult learner.

Formal teaching

A formal teaching strategy will consist principally of asking your trainee to perform his learning task in a prescribed manner.

Your trainee, therefore, will be encouraged to memorize information, to imitate a model example, to adhere to a prescribed doctrine and to follow strict guidelines. Rigid parrot-fashion learning, however, will not normally be appropriate for adult vocational training.

Formal teaching will usually only apply in a hypnotherapy context when a given set of rules must be strictly followed. If your trainee, however, rigidly follows an entrenched set of rules for therapeutic practice then he may be robbed of the spontaneous, flexible and creative approach which will be essential for professional working practice.

You should employ formal methodology only very sparingly when necessary in the early stages of hypnotherapy practice training but, in the fullness of time, you should invite your trainee to think creatively on his feet because this faculty will be required of him in the professional world.

Teaching strategy evaluation

You will need to review your training strategy objectives in order to assess whether the intended outcome for your learner has been achieved.

This process of evaluating your teaching strategy objectives and measuring these against the final outcome will be a delicate balancing-act for you which must conclude satisfactorily for your trainee.

Throughout your entire training programme you will need to decide whether the real learning outcome actually meets your expectations and the intended goal for your learners. You will also need to debate whether the goal for your trainees has been attained at the end of each session as well as in the final reckoning.

You will, furthermore, need to consider what may occur in the future in terms of the overall learning benefit to your prospective practitioner. There may well be a delayed outcome for your trainee who will be intending to work in professional practice but this eventuality may not be realized until long after your training course has been completed.

TEACHING STRATEGY ASSIGNMENT

Answer the questions shown below about teaching strategy, pose any further questions which might arise during this process and decide what action, if any, you propose to take as a result of your findings.

- Do you appreciate the need for a teaching strategy which will fulfil your course objectives?

- Are you fully aware of your role as a strategist whose task will be to organize the training environment for your trainee?
- Might an episodic teaching strategy be the most appropriate solution when training adult learners who may have busy lives?
- When might a continuous teaching strategy be appropriate for your trainee?
- Why is trainee-centred learning so important for adult vocational training?
- What might be the merits of curriculum-centred learning for your trainee?
- Would you consider any occasion when a formal teaching strategy might be appropriate for your course-participants?
- How might you employ an informal teaching strategy to the greatest advantage with your learner?
- Why might an informal teaching strategy be the most effective for vocational training with an adult learner?
- In what ways might you reflectively evaluate your teaching strategy objectives?

Teaching Methodology

Teaching methodology principles

You must employ the most appropriate teaching methodology for your hypnotherapy learner so that he can effectively acquire his knowledge and skill (see Figure 22: *Teaching Methodology*).

The teaching methodology which you are most likely to utilize for hypnotherapy tuition will be group presentation, group demonstration, group discussion, group questioning, supervised practice and project-work.

Always ensure that your teaching methodology can be varied so that you will be able to provide your trainee with opportunity for both active learning pursuit and passive learning activity during his learning experience.

Figure 22: Teaching Methodology

Teaching Activity	Teaching Application	Learning Process
Group presentation	Tutor provides a seminar-style or a lecture-style presentation	Passive
Group demonstration	Tutor demonstrates a practical skill	Passive
Group discussion	Trainee undertakes a problem-solving task Trainee undertakes a strategic planning task Trainee engages in a therapy-style dialogue Trainee provides a report	Active/Passive
Group questioning	Trainee assesses his own learning Tutor assesses trainee's learning Tutor assesses teaching methodology	Active/Passive
Supervised practice	Trainee applies learned principles Trainee assesses his own learning	Active
Project-work	Trainee undertakes a problem-solving task Trainee undertakes an independent research task Trainee assesses his own learning	Active

GROUP PRESENTATION

A group presentation session can be utilized effectively when you need to impart a knowledge component to your training group as an easy and efficient means of putting information across speedily.

A group presentation can be employed for conveying basic information, providing a case-study example, explaining a given therapeutic technique or delivering basic instructions to your training group. A group hypnotherapy session might also be classified as a form of group presentation.

You will almost certainly need to present information to your trainees in order to impart knowledge either as a seminar-style presentation or as a lecture-style presentation to your training group. The seminar-style presentation will cater for a small group or a medium-sized group during which you can usually make direct contact with each group-participant. The lecture-style presentation will be required for imparting matter to a large training group with minimal direct interaction with your audience.

The seminar-style presentation will obviously be the most appropriate presentation approach when undertaking hypnotherapy training because of the special needs of the group-participants. You can, by this means, attend to the special requirements of your trainee yet make effective use of time by being able to convey the subject-matter to your training group as a whole.

Your group presentation should be well structured with an introductory component, a development section and a conclusion so that your trainee can easily follow your line of argument.

Make contact with your listeners during your presentation whenever possible in order to ensure that each learner can follow the essentials of the subject-matter.

Because any form of group presentation will usually be a relatively passive form of learning activity for your trainees you might be advised to ensure that your presentation is not lengthy and, if at all possible, that audience participation can become an integral part of your teaching methodology.

You should also endeavour to enhance your presentation with training resources and possibly encourage your trainees to take notes in order to provide some active learning endeavour. Any presentation which you conduct can definitely be enhanced by utilizing teaching resources, such as visual aids or handouts, both as a means of clarifying and reinforcing the subject-matter as well as injecting interest into your trainee's learning experience.

GROUP DEMONSTRATION

A group demonstration session can be utilized effectively when you are imparting a skill component to your training group.

When teaching your trainee to acquire and to develop a practical skill it will be essential for you to conduct a demonstration of that skill which he can observe in action first hand. Your trainee, by this means, will be able to observe, for instance, the way in which a typical client-session can be conducted or a given therapeutic technique could be undertaken.

Your trainee can, consequently, observe the therapeutic process in action, the way in which the therapeutic procedure could be undertaken and the specific techniques involved in practice. Your trainee may also observe skeletal guidelines, note correct procedures, glean ideas and receive pointers which he can later put into practice himself. Typically you might select a candidate or ask for a volunteer from your audience who would be willing to act as a practice client for your group demonstration.

When demonstrating a skill to your trainees you should ensure that all learners can clearly see what you are doing and can hear what you are saying. You must also guarantee that each course-participant can easily follow the steps and the route which you might be taking during your demonstration. You can ensure the effectiveness of your demonstration by stating your objectives in advance and later summarizing the steps which you have taken once it has been completed. If at all possible you may also be able to analyse the procedure which you are adopting during your live demonstration.

Because a practical group demonstration will be a relatively passive learning activity for your trainee it will, by itself, be an inadequate means for him to develop his skill unless he can swiftly put what he has observed into practice himself – preferably immediately afterwards.

GROUP DISCUSSION

A group discussion session can be utilized in order to permit your trainee to share his views and to debate his training topics. Your hypnotherapy training programme may lend itself to regular group discussion sessions in which both active learning activity and passive learning processes can occur.

You could utilize group discussion for a problem-solving activity, a brainstorming forum and when your trainee is formulating his plans for a therapeutic practice session. You could also organize group discussion by way of a group-therapy style dialogue for the personal development of your trainee. A group discussion can, furthermore, be employed for a feedback reporting session following your trainee's practical learning activity.

A group discussion session may be a scheduled activity which might be tutor-led or it may occur as an impromptu trainee-led session which might arise as result of another training activity.

The advantage of the group discussion session will be to provide an opening for each member of your training group to make a positive contribution and for all to exchange views, convey ideas and share experiences.

You should, of course, ensure that your group discussion will not become dominated by a single group-member and that all your course-participants can be given an opportunity – and, indeed, encouraged – to contribute significantly. During any form of group discussion, therefore, your trainee should have an equal opportunity of having a voice and then getting his questions answered satisfactorily.

GROUP QUESTIONING

A group questioning session can be utilized in order assess your trainee or to allow for a feedback opportunity for him.

You may find it expedient to include much opportunity for group questioning within your hypnotherapy training programme in which both active learning activity and passive learning awareness can take place.

Group questioning in a question-and-answer format may be employed in order to afford your trainee a chance to reflect on his learning experience and to seek further clarification of his subject-matter whenever necessary. Your trainee, for instance, may be more than curious about working in professional practice and this topic alone may generate a flood of questions.

During a group questioning session each trainee should be given an opportunity to ask a question if the discussion might be of a general nature. Always ensure, therefore, that your trainees can hear all questions posed from the floor and, if necessary, repeat each enquiry so that you and your audience are clear about what is being asked.

You might also employ a group questioning strategy when you wish to informally assess your trainee's comprehension of the knowledge and the skill which he has acquired. This ploy will then provide you with valuable feedback about the way in which you might need to recapitulate a given topic in order to ensure that your trainee's learning has been completed comprehensively and effectively.

When your group questioning is being conducted for assessment purposes then each trainee could be questioned informally so that he can be assessed as an individual and, simultaneously, the training group's performance can be measured as a whole.

Supervised practice

A supervised practice session can be utilized in order to allow your trainee to develop his skill in a nurturing environment.

Your trainee will need to practice the skill of conducting a therapeutic session with appropriate use of professional practice methodology with his client. It will, consequently, be essential for you to ask your trainee to conduct a number of observed practice sessions as an active learning experience during his hypnotherapy training programme.

Typically your trainee's supervised practice will be prefaced by a demonstration of the technique in question coupled with the provision of some planning guidelines. In the early stages of your trainee's journey you may wish to provide much in the way of demonstration and planning assistance prior his practice session.

As your trainee's learning progresses, however, you may find that it will be sufficient to outline the therapeutic methodology in principle before throwing him in at the deep end. Your trainee, by this means, will be building on his existing learning while his practice confidence is being cemented throughout his learning experience.

During any observation of your trainee's practical work you may need to assist him gently and unobtrusively with any difficulty and you should note any aspects of his work which could tactfully be enhanced. Because undertaking practical skill-based work will be a creative activity you should, however, ensure that you stimulate your trainee's enthusiasm, praise him for his efforts and cultivate his unique style.

Therapeutic practice is a creative and highly personal activity and, therefore, you should be working towards nurturing your trainee's emergent skills in order to allow him to blossom with minimal intervention from his tutor.

PROJECT-WORK

A project-work assignment can be utilized in order to allow your trainee to undertake his own independent and self-directed study.

You may wish to ask your trainee to undertake some form of project-work assignment as an integral part of his learning experience and, by this means, you will be engaging him in his own self-motivated and self-organized learning experience.

Project-work during your trainee's course attendance may, for instance, take the form of devising a script for delivery during a practice session or as fodder for group discussion. Your trainee might even be asked to deliver a talk to your training group.

Project-work may also take the form of a homework assignment in which your trainee will be requested to answer some set questions and, perhaps, to undertake independent research in the process. A homework assignment may entail answering a series of multiple-choice questions or could involve writing an essay in order to measure your trainee's understanding of factual knowledge so that he can consolidate his learning.

A homework project could also entail asking your trainee to conduct a therapeutic session with a practice client on which he can report in writing or debate verbally within a group discussion session. Your trainee's homework assignment may be formally assessed by you or it may simply serve to enlighten your trainee about his own progress.

When assigning project-work tasks – during which your trainee may be working relatively unaided – you should ensure that it will be abundantly clear what will be expected of him. Your trainee's project assignment might, therefore, be requested by you both in writing and verbally. You will, furthermore, need to gauge whether it would be appropriate for your trainee to undertake his project-work as an independent study task or, alternatively, under your close direction.

TEACHING METHODOLOGY ASSIGNMENT

Answer the questions shown below about teaching methodology, pose any further questions which might arise during this process and decide what action, if any, you propose to take as a result of your findings.

- Do you fully appreciate the function of employing a varied selection of teaching activity for your trainee?
- Can you identify the teaching activity which will constitute an active learning pursuit and a passive learning interest for your trainee?

- What are the advantages and the disadvantages of the seminar-style group presentation as compared with the lecture-style group presentation?

- Why will a group demonstration be such an essential feature of your trainee's skill development process?

- What procedures will you adopt when conducting a group demonstration for your course-participants?

- What methodology would you employ when facilitating a group discussion with your training group?

- In what ways might you utilize group questioning opportunities as a teaching ploy?

- In what ways might your trainee benefit from supervised practice?

- How will you approach the task of supervising practice sessions with your trainee?

- What guidelines will you provide for your trainee when he undertakes a project-work assignment?

Teaching Resource Utilization

Teaching resource utilization principles

Teaching resources and learning aids will be of vital assistance to you when imparting knowledge and developing skill in your trainee (see Figure 23: *Teaching Resources*).

Teaching resources can greatly assist your learner to comprehend the subject-matter, to maintain his interest and to make his learning process a multi-sensory experience. Training resources can often transform a passive learning activity into an active learning process for your trainee particularly when group discussion can be generated.

The main teaching resources which you could utilize may take the form of audio-visual equipment, presentation equipment, internet resources and handout material.

A note of the teaching resources which you intend to utilize could be included as part of your documented training session plans.

FIGURE 23: TEACHING RESOURCES

TEACHING ACTIVITY	TEACHING RESOURCES	LEARNING AIDS
Group presentation	Slide projector Whiteboard Flipchart	Handout material Stationery and writing materials Internet resources
Group demonstration	Slide projector Whiteboard Flipchart	Handout material Stationery and writing materials Internet resources
Group discussion	Slide projector Whiteboard Flipchart	Handout material Stationery and writing materials Internet resources
Group questioning	Slide projector Whiteboard Flipchart	Handout material Stationery and writing materials Internet resources

Supervised practice	Whiteboard	Handout material
	Flipchart	Stationery and writing materials
Project-work	Whiteboard	Handout material
	Flipchart	Published literature
		Internet resources

AUDIO-VISUAL EQUIPMENT

Audio-visual equipment of the high-tech variety can become an essential aid to your teaching activity. A set of projected slides can be used, for instance, in order to illustrate your group presentation, group demonstration and group discussion.

A talk can be eye-catchingly illustrated with a slide projector linked to a computer with presentation software. The presentation software will render your slides attractive, easy to compile and a delight for your trainees to behold. You can also utilize presentation software in order to give your whole training programme a designed theme and, once created, a set of slides can be repeatedly used as a permanent teaching resource.

When compiling a set of presentation slides always ensure that you do not over-crowd any slide by attempting to give too much information or too much detail. Your slides should be a prompt or a summary of your presentation not a detailed treatise.

You should, of course, adopt wording and employ diagrams which are clear, legible and unambiguous. Use an attractive typestyle and an effective point-size in the lettering of your wording. Utilize striking designs, colourful diagrams and clear illustrations whenever possible as a supplement to the information which you are imparting to your trainees.

Do not, however, become over-zealous in terms of flashy special-effects when utilizing presentation software for teaching purposes – such razzmatazz might be more suitable for a sales-pitch.

Presentation equipment

Presentation equipment can constitute a relatively low-cost and ever-ready medium for enhancing your group presentation, group demonstration, group discussion and group questioning.

A flipchart or a whiteboard may, therefore, be a constant source of assistance to you during your teaching delivery.

A flipchart with an easel and a supply of coloured pens can be used as a convenient teaching aid which can be brought into play at any given moment during your training programme. Your argument could be built up and developed, for example, using a flipchart on which you can make notes, highlight important points or create diagrams when imparting knowledge to your trainees.

You can also make full use of colour when illustrating points with a flipchart.

A flipchart will be of benefit if you wish to refer back to a previous discussion at a later date and, therefore, it will constitute a semi-permanent teaching record.

The lettering on any flipchart sheet should be readable from a distance and should be clearly visible even to those sitting furthest away. Do not overcrowd your flipchart sheets and do not allow it to become a scrappy jotter for any random thoughts as they occur to you in the live training session. Be ever vigilant, therefore, of keeping the subject-matter relevant and neatly presented on your flipchart.

A wipe-dry whiteboard with a number of marker pens can be used to assist your training delivery by providing a semi-permanent aid on which you can readily make notes, provide a summary or present a colourful diagram. Whiteboard technology has evolved to the extent that an interactive whiteboard can now be linked to your computer and used as a three-dimensional medium.

Again do not fall into the trap of using your whiteboard as a general notepad which can become a patchwork quilt of scribbles if you are not well disciplined. Remember that the whiteboard will always be on view and that, therefore, its contents will be a permanent record in the eyes of your trainee until it has been cleared. Bear in mind, moreover, that the conventional whiteboard will need to be cleared before it can be reused and that only semi-permanent markers are suitable for this medium.

INTERNET RESOURCES

Internet resources can provide an abundant and endless source of information and illustration which you can utilize very effectively in your teaching.

A video film or an audio recording can be invaluable when presenting a given idea or when providing a case-study example for your trainee. You might utilize a training video from the internet, for instance, which can be projected on to a screen linked to your computer in order to illustrate your group presentation, group demonstration or group discussion.

When showing a video film or listening to an audio recording always remember to introduce the medium, point out features to watch for and then summarize and discuss what has been viewed or heard afterwards in order to obtain maximum benefit from this form of learning aid for your trainee.

The internet can also become a valuable resource for your trainee who might be required to undertake independent research when completing a written assignment.

HANDOUT MATERIAL

Handout material can be an ideal way of providing your trainee with a summary – or even the complete picture – of the subject-matter which he will be endeavouring to acquire.

It will usually be advisable for you to provide your trainee with some form of documentation which can support his learning process. Handout material can range from a simple printout of your slide presentation to a full written account of your subject-matter for the entire course.

Should any part of your course programme call for a home-study component then full documentation will be essential to your trainee's learning process.

A summary of your slide presentation can usually be easily catered for with a handout for your trainees – perhaps taken from the slides which you have shown during your group presentation, group demonstration or group discussion. A short summary can, alternatively, be provided of any talks which you deliver to your learner when imparting knowledge. When developing a skill in your trainee you might wish to provide a sample hypnotic text or a step-by-step set of practice guidelines in written form.

Any handout material which you issue to your trainee should, of course, be well written, easy to understand, illustrated with diagrams when appropriate and free of any typographical errors. Such material may, therefore, take some considerable time for you to prepare at your course planning stage and you may also need to invest further time in keeping your material up-to-date.

TEACHING RESOURCE UTILIZATION ASSIGNMENT

Answer the questions shown below about teaching resource utilization, pose any further questions which might arise during this process and decide what action, if any, you propose to take as a result of your findings.

- Are you making full use of visual resources in order to support and to enhance the learning experience for your trainee?

- In what ways could you utilize slide-projection and film-projection equipment in support of your group presentation, group demonstration and group discussion session?

- Can you ensure that your projected slides are a summary of your presentation rather than a comprehensive treatise?

- Is the wording of your slide-presentation material utterly clear, legible and unambiguous when illustrating important concepts?

- Can the wording on your flipchart or your whiteboard be seen by all your audience-members?

- Can you make effective use of diagrams on your flipchart or your whiteboard as a valuable teaching resource?
- Can you encourage your trainee to undertake research on the internet when appropriate?
- Have you fully exploited the internet as a teaching resource?
- What do you intend to provide in the form of handout material for your trainee?
- Can you review your handout material in order to ensure that the wording and the diagrams are eye-catching, clear, unambiguous and free of any typographical errors?

TEACHING THEORY APPLICATION

TEACHING THEORY APPLICATION PRINCIPLES

You can apply the principles of teaching when conducting your training programme by ensuring that you follow a meaningful set of guidelines when you are assisting your trainee with his learning experience (see Figure 24: *TEACHING PRINCIPLE APPLICATION*).

A typical set of training guidelines might include a process whereby you state your learning intention and then convey the basic principles in respect of the knowledge and the skill which your trainee may be asked to acquire.

Your next step might then be to evaluate the outcome of your trainee's learning experience with a view to assessing his performance, obtaining feedback from him and then measuring your own teaching strategy and training methodology accordingly.

When applying learning principles you will need to undergo a self-reflective process so that you can truly assess your trainee and, simultaneously, you can evaluate your own performance as a tutor.

FIGURE 24: TEACHING PRINCIPLE APPLICATION

TEACHING PRINCIPLE	TEACHING ACTIVITY
State learning intention	Group presentation
Summarize general topic principles	Group presentation Group demonstration Group discussion Group questioning
Convey practical guidelines	Group presentation Group demonstration Group discussion Group questioning
Assess tangible outcome	Group discussion Group questioning Supervised practice Project-work

Assess trainee performance	Group discussion Group questioning Supervised practice Project-work
Provide trainee feedback	Group discussion Group questioning Supervised practice Project-work
Monitor teaching standards	Group discussion Group questioning Supervised practice Project-work

LEARNING INTENTIONS

You might introduce a new learning topic by outlining initially what you intend your trainee to acquire in terms of his knowledge and skill acquisition.

You will probably convey your overall learning intention to your trainee at the start of any group presentation or group demonstration.

You may, for instance, describe a new therapeutic technique, state its purpose, suggest ways in which it could be applied in practice and outline its historical development.

When introducing factual subject-matter you could, moreover, provide a broad-brush overview and then highlight the points which you later intend to cover.

TOPIC PRESENTATION

You can now begin the process of conveying the underlying general principles of the subject-matter to your trainees.

When presenting fresh practical work you could outline the general concept and the purpose of the skill which you will expect your trainee to develop. You might, consequently, provide an outline of the general skeletal framework of a given therapeutic technique before demonstrating this methodology to your trainees.

Knowledge acquisition could be tackled by giving a group presentation illustrated with visual aids which will detail the subject-matter to be acquired by your trainee.

Whenever you are imparting information to your trainee you should always allow him time to assimilate the subject-matter and provide ample opportunity for him to ask pertinent questions.

Practical guidelines

Your next step may be to provide your trainee with some practical guidelines in order to assist him with the application of his learning in practice.

When your trainee is in the process of acquiring skill you may now wish to summarize the steps you have taken during your practical demonstration of a given therapeutic technique. You might also ask your trainee to devise a plan of action for his future reference.

When your trainee is being asked to acquire knowledge you may find that you will need to summarize the main points which you have initially presented or even to recapitulate the whole topic. Often a group discussion or a group questioning strategy can be employed in order to elicit suggestions from your trainee about the varying ways of tackling a given problem and, simultaneously, you can take the opportunity of assessing his comprehension of the subject-matter.

Tangible outcomes

You will now need to assess the actual tangible outcome of your trainee's learning experience. You should discover whether a wide discrepancy exists between your intended learning objectives and the tangible result of your teaching so that you can take steps to bridge any gaps.

You could request your trainee to put his practical learning to the test or to apply his theoretical knowledge in a given situation so that he can decide whether his learning has been beneficial. Your trainee might, for instance, be asked to put his theoretical knowledge of a given therapeutic technique into live practice so that you can assess whether your learning objectives have been met.

TRAINEE PERFORMANCE

You will next need to evaluate the performance of your trainee in order to ensure that he has satisfactorily acquired the necessary knowledge or skill.

You could, for instance, make a diagnosis on the basis of your trainee's performance, assess his future training needs, rectify any of his limitations and plan his additional training accordingly.

Often a lengthy review process will be called for following any supervised practice sessions not only in order to allow a free exchange of ideas among the members of your training group but also so that you can assess the effectiveness of each trainee's learning experience.

A somewhat formal assessment strategy might be more appropriate for gauging the extent of your trainee's theoretical learning.

TRAINEE FEEDBACK

Once you have observed your trainee's application of his knowledge by supervising his project-work and his skill by overseeing his practical work you can then provide him with constructive feedback as necessary.

You should ensure that you can in some way report back to your trainee about the conclusions which you have drawn about his performance and his overall progress.

This feedback-reporting approach should serve to show your trainee the progress he has made, to reinforce his learning, to optimize his strengths and to kindle his motivation rather than to deflate his self-esteem.

If there is a serious mismatch between your learning intentions and your trainee's tangible learning outcome then you may need to consider the way in which you will rectify this discrepancy. Your trainee, for instance, may need some private tuition or you might wish to allot some additional time for revision and recapitulation.

TEACHING STANDARDS

You ought finally to reflect on and to adjust your own teaching standards and your personal performance as necessary and, perhaps, then rethink your training methodology and revise your learning objectives accordingly.

You should take a sober and honest look at what your trainee has achieved and your key role in the teaching-learning equation so that you can ensure that he will develop and that he can achieve competence to the required standard.

When your trainee has been acquiring practical skill you may need to assess whether you have successfully managed to develop his skill to an acceptable level suitable for professional practice.

When your trainee has been acquiring knowledge you will need to satisfy yourself that he has understood, he can regurgitate and he can apply the subject-matter appropriately. Should your trainee fall short of the mark then you may well wish to recapitulate or, even, to present the subject-matter again in a different way.

TEACHING THEORY APPLICATION ASSIGNMENT

Answer the questions shown below about teaching theory application, pose any further questions which might arise during this process and decide what action, if any, you propose to take as a result of your findings.

- Do you appreciate the way in which you can apply the principles of teaching when assisting your hypnotherapy practitioners?
- Do you normally state your trainee's future learning intentions when introducing a new topic?
- Can you summarize your trainee's learning intention succinctly so that he will be left in no doubt whatsoever about the aim of his learning experience?
- In what ways will you present the general topic principles of what you intend to convey to your trainee?
- In what ways will you deliver practice guidance to your trainee?
- By what means can you accurately assess your trainee's practical performance of any given therapeutic technique?
- Are you keenly aware of the way in which your trainee can perform a practical skill competently?
- In what ways can you provide your trainee with constructive feedback about his learning experience?
- Are you able to make a true evaluation of your skill as a teacher and to rectify any of your shortcomings accordingly?
- Do you appreciate that you may need to review your teaching strategy in the light of your learning outcome for your trainee?

Teaching Programme Evaluation

Teaching Programme Evaluation Principles

You should continually evaluate your training programme in order you ensure that you can optimize the learning experience for your trainee (see Figure 25: *Teaching Programme Evaluation*).

The evaluation of your training programme will essentially require you to keep a constant watchful eye on your learner's performance, your learning objectives and your teaching methodology.

Your work as a course tutor will consist of a pre-delivery stage, a delivery stage and a review stage in connection with your training programme which should all be evaluated as an ongoing procedure. Your self-reflective role as a tutor will pay dividends for the success of your training programme and the welfare of your trainee.

You will need to select the appropriate instructional techniques, the training activity and the training resources which you will employ for your learner and then deliver your training programme according to your initial plans.

You will find that your pre-delivery activity will blend into the delivery phase of your training programme as a continual monitoring process.

When delivering your training programme you should, of course, continually gauge the effectiveness of your teaching methodology and your learner's training activity.

Your teaching methodology may often need to undergo a radical transformation during any training course even though the overall learning aim for your trainee should remain constant. Your role as the orchestrator of your trainee's learning experience should come under scrutiny constantly so that you can make any necessary fine-tuning adjustments before disaster strikes.

The final delivery and the post-delivery phases of your course will consist of reviewing your teaching work both while your live training programme is taking place as well as afterwards so that your discoveries can be utilized in the future as appropriate.

FIGURE 25: TEACHING PROGRAMME EVALUATION

LEARNING STAGE	PRE-DELIVERY	DELIVERY	POST-DELIVERY
Learner evaluation	Assess trainee's experience, ability and potential	Assess trainee's performance and provide feedback report	Assess trainee's performance during supervisory interaction
Learning objective evaluation	Set learning objectives and intended outcomes	Monitor learning objectives and tangible outcomes	Evaluate learning objectives during course review process
Teaching methodology evaluation	Select teaching activity and training resources	Monitor teaching activity and training resources	Evaluate teaching methodology during course review process

LEARNER EVALUATION

During the pre-delivery phase of your training programme your remit will to be set your learning objectives and to assess your trainee's past experience, his ability and his potential in order to ensure that he can meet the demands of your training course.

During your training course delivery you will need to carefully monitor the competence and the performance of your trainee in order to ensure that you can keep your learning objectives on track. If you find that your trainee has been lagging behind because he has been overwhelmed by the competence-level of your course content or the volume of work which will be required then you may need to take some remedial action as a result.

You should ensure that your learner can keep track of his own learning process so that he can be assured that his learning will effectively be taking place. Your trainee, consequently, will probably need constant feedback and confirmation of his learning achievements.

Both formal and informal assessment can go a long way towards meeting these demands so that your trainee can be assured that his learning experience will be suitable for his purpose. The adult learner, of course, will usually be able to make his own personal assessment of his learning experience.

Learning objective evaluation

Once you have formulated your overall learning objectives for your training programme you will need to ensure that your plans are largely being fulfilled.

Your teaching methodology can, however, be continually monitored and adjusted in order to ensure that your learning objectives are being met by your trainee and that your training programme schedule will be on target.

There can be a fine balance between setting and attaining learning objectives and then making the necessary modifications throughout your course delivery in order to allow for any discrepancies.

You could, for instance, have misjudged your trainee during his initial prospective learner assessment and then, consequently, you will need to make alternations to your teaching methodology in order to accommodate your own miscalculation.

Your trainee, moreover, may simply not be sufficiently motivated, inherently incapable or not dedicated enough to meet the demands of your training programme – in which case some modifications may need to be made to your teaching activity and your trainee's circumstances accordingly.

TEACHING METHODOLOGY EVALUATION

You will need to continually evaluate your own performance both during and after a training course so that you can maximise your teaching effectiveness and can ensure the success of your trainee.

You will need to assess not only the choice of your training methodology but also the usefulness of training resources and the way in which you make effective use of time.

Teaching programme evaluation assignment

Answer the questions shown below about teaching programme evaluation, pose any further questions which might arise during this process and decide what action, if any, you propose to take as a result of your findings.

- To what extent have your learning objectives been successfully realized by your trainee?

- Have you made an accurate assessment of your trainee prior to the commencement of his learning experience?

- Have you made an accurate assessment of your trainee during his learning experience?

- Is your instructional methodology appropriate for your trainee?

- Will you need to make any modifications to the way in which you might deliver your training programme for your trainee?

- Is your teaching methodology in any way falling short of your expectation?

- Does your trainee receive adequate feedback about his learning success?

- Does your trainee believe that he has achieved his true learning potential?
- Will you need to remedy any shortfall in your trainee's learning performance?
- Can you ensure that you are clearly able to demonstrate to your trainee the effectiveness of his learning experience?

Teaching & Learning Models

Teaching-learning models

A teaching-learning model is an outline framework which will describe the process of learning and the steps which you will need to take in order to ensure that your trainee can effectively acquire his knowledge and skill.

A number of educators have put forward theories of teaching-learning for conventional state education and for private alternative education both of which you could consider as background information for your hypnotherapy training practice.

Basic teaching model

The basic teaching model was devised by the educational psychologist Robert Glaser (1921-2012) whose work has made a significant contribution to teacher education and training programmes (see Figure 26: BASIC TEACHING MODEL).

The basic teaching model will consider the way in which various components of the learning-teaching equation can inter-relate.

The basic teaching model identifies four major elements which interact in order to facilitate your trainee's learning experience. The four major dovetailing components of the learning process are designated as instructional objectives, entry behaviour, instructional procedures and trainee-performance assessment.

You must first set instructional objectives and then assess the level of ability of your trainee in order to be able to formulate your teaching strategy and to select appropriate teaching methodology. Once your programme of study has been designed your trainee will then need to be assessed in order to evaluate the effectiveness of his learning experience and to monitor the teaching methodology which you have employed.

The basic teaching model has been highly influential in differentiating between the learning process and the teaching activity of the tutor. This teaching-learning model, therefore, will focus on the teaching process with a heavy emphasis on the tutor's decision-making ability and his problem-solving competence.

FIGURE 26: BASIC TEACHING MODEL

Teaching Component	Component Characteristics
Instructional objectives	Tutor sets intended learning objectives for trainee
Entry behaviour	Tutor assesses trainee's level of ability, prior knowledge, previous experience and inherent attributes
Instructional procedures	Tutor selects teaching methodology, utilizes training resources and organizes learning environment
Performance assessment	Tutor evaluates trainee's competence and performance ability

CYCLE OF LEARNING EXPERIENCE MODEL

The cycle of learning experience model was devised by the educational theorist David Kolb (1939-) who also advocated experiential learning theory, promoted reflective learning theory and formulated learning styles for conceptualization, reflection, assimilation and experimentation (see Figure 27: CYCLE OF LEARNING EXPERIENCE MODEL).

The cycle of learning experience model has been based on the premise that your trainee's learning experience will be influenced by his inherent ability, his past experience and the way in which he interacts with his environment.

The cycle of learning model, which was refined by Peter Honey and Alan Mumford, specifies four distinct phases of the learning process each of which will be interdependent.

Your trainee must first undergo a concrete experience and he must then reflect on his learning process. Your trainee can now conceptualize his learning experience and finally he can actively experiment with his newly acquired knowledge and skill.

The cycle of learning experience model, therefore, will engaged your trainee in becoming an activist, a reflector, a theorist and a pragmatist.

FIGURE 27: CYCLE OF LEARNING EXPERIENCE MODEL

LEARNING STAGE	LEARNING ACTIVITY	TRAINEE FOCUS
Concrete experience	Trainee undergoes his learning experience	Activist
Reflective observation	Trainee reflects on his learning experience	Reflector
Abstract conceptualization	Trainee draws conclusions about his learning experience	Theorist
Active experimentation	Trainee experiments constructively with his learning experience	Pragmatist

ANTHROPOSOPHICAL TEACHING MODEL

The philosopher Rudolf Steiner (1861-1925) devised a teaching model based on anthroposophical principles as an alternative education methodology (see Figure 28: *ANTHROPOSOPHICAL TEACHING MODEL*).

The anthroposophical teaching model aims to develop your trainee's independent thinking, his clear logic and his appreciation of sensory experience. Anthroposophical philosophy advocates your trainee's personal growth potential which can be brought about by the development of his perception, imagination, inspiration and intuition. According to anthroposophical theory your learner can thus acquire the ability to live a spiritually oriented lifestyle.

The anthroposophical teaching model will consider education as a number of spheres of learning experience and has identified three major personality types which your trainee will exhibit. The theory which underpins the anthroposophical teaching model is that your trainee will exhibit a dominant personality type which will be inclined towards thinking processes, feeling sensitivity or willing action.

If your trainee becomes a thinking type he will usually be inclined towards logical, intellectual and imaginative thinking processes. The thinking type, therefore, will probably want to adopt a scientific approach to his learning experience. The thinking type will usually relate to a critical-appraisal learning strategy and a theoretical learning style.

If your trainee becomes a feeling type he will usually be inclined towards sensory experience, emotive reaction and spiritual awareness in his approach to life. The feeling type, therefore, will probably adopt a creative and an artistic approach to his learning experience. The feeling type will probably relate best to a self-awareness learning approach and a reflective learning style.

If your trainee becomes a willing type he will usually be inclined towards self-stimulating action and may be enthusiastic, deliberate and methodical in his approach to life. The willing type, therefore, will probably adopt an active and a productive approach to his learning experience. The willing type will usually respond best to a behavioural learning approach and an experimental learning style.

FIGURE 28: ANTHROPOSOPHICAL TEACHING MODEL

PERSONALITY TYPE	CHARACTER TRAITS	LEARNING INFLUENCES	CAREER-ORIENTATION
Thinking	Logical and imaginative	Conscious awareness	Scientist
Feeling	Sensitive, emotive and spiritual	Conscious and unconscious awareness	Artist

Willing	Enthusiastic, deliberate and methodical	Unconscious awareness	Craftsman

TEACHING AND LEARNING MODELS ASSIGNMENT

Answer the questions shown below about teaching and learning models, pose any further questions which might arise during this process and decide what action, if any, you propose to take as a result of your findings.

- In what ways might the basic teaching model be applicable to your training programme?

- In what ways might you balance and reconcile the formulation of your learning objectives and the assessment of your potential trainee?

- In what ways would your training delivery and your teaching methodology take into account the ability and the potential of your trainee in the light of your planned learning objectives?

- Will any modifications need to be made to your teaching programme once you have assessed your trainee's learning performance?

- What is your opinion of the cycle of learning experience model and could you apply this theory in practice?

- Can you see evidence of the way in which your trainee will undergo the process of concrete experience, reflective observation, abstract conceptualization and active experimentation according to the cycle of learning experience model?

- In what ways could you apply an anthroposophical approach to your teaching programme?

- Does the concept of the anthroposophical teaching model appeal to you as a teacher of hypnotherapy practitioners?

- Can you identify your trainee as a thinking type, a feeling type or a willing type according to the anthroposophical model of teaching?

- Could you design your teaching strategy according to the anthroposophical classification of your trainee?

SUPERVISORY PRINCIPLES

THE SUPERVISOR

SUPERVISORY PRINCIPLES

The nature of supervision will be to provide a safe sanctuary for your hypnotherapy supervisee in which he can freely discuss his practice methodology and he can develop his professional career.

The supervisory process will consists of a threefold element of providing professional support, enhancing professional development and safeguarding the wellbeing of both your supervisee and his client.

THE SUPERVISORY ROLE

Your supervisory function will be to consider the psychological wellbeing of your supervisee by understanding him as an evolving practitioner and by monitoring his supervisee-client interaction.

Your supervisory role will essentially be one of nurturing your supervisee as a working professional and overseeing his professional practice in order to ensure that he can safely and ethical undertake his work. You should thus endeavour to assess the relationship formed between your supervisee and his client in order to oil the wheels of his professional therapeutic practice. You must, therefore, to be able to gently orchestrate the work of your supervisee so that he can function safely and ethically in his workplace.

The nurturing and mentoring elements of your role as a supervisor will be akin to hypnotherapy training and therapeutic intervention.

SUPERVISORY ATTRIBUTES

You will need to possess a number of personal attributes in order to fulfil your supervisory function of nurturing, safeguarding and developing your supervisee as a professional practitioner.

You will need to be caring and empathetic to the needs of your supervisee as a working specialist. You should, therefore, be equipped to understand the emotively taxing elements of your supervisee's work and be fully equipped to assist him in surmounting any personal obstacles to professional success. You will, consequently, need to understand the therapeutic process in depth as a practitioner and you must be able to speak authoritatively from your extensive first-hand experience.

You should be able to view the relationship between your supervisee and his client from a distant perspective so that you can gain a realistic overview of the therapeutic encounter even though you can only behold one side of the coin.

You will be required to work in the interests of your supervisee by guiding and steering him through his working practice in such a way that he can become confident, successful, effective and ethical as a hypnotherapy practitioner.

Your supervisory skills can, of course, also be employed in order to assist any other practitioner in the field of alternative therapy and complementary medicine – despite the fact that your specialism will be in hypnotherapy practice.

THE SUPERVISOR ASSIGNMENT

Answer the questions shown below about the supervisor, pose any further questions which might arise during this process and decide what action, if any, you propose to take as a result of your findings.

- Do you fully understand your role as a clinical supervisor?

- Can you outline the function of the supervisory process?
- What should be the nature of the supervisory environment for your supervisee?
- What might be the intrinsic needs of your supervisee as a professional practitioner?
- In what ways can you offer personal support to your supervisee?
- Are you able to identify your supervisee's requirement for assistance with his practice management?
- Do you realistically possess the appropriate competence in order to assist your supervisee?
- Can you take a complete overview of your supervisee's work in order to assist him and his client?
- Do you appreciate that supervisory work can be akin to both teaching and therapeutic intervention?
- What personal qualities would you require as a supervisor of hypnotherapy practitioners?

Supervisory Enquiry

Supervisory enquiry principles

Your initial task will be to familiarize yourself with the way in which your supervisee works when you meet him for an initial exploratory session. You will thus need to make enquiries in order to assess your supervisee's background and to understand his unique circumstances.

Often the issues which your supervisee will bring into your consulting room will be those of his relationship with his client, his perceived degree of professional competence and any transference or counter-transference issues which may be arising for him.

You should endeavour, therefore, to assess the experience and the competence-level of your supervisee and to understand him both as a working professional and as an individual.

You will, furthermore, be required to evaluate the therapeutic relationship which your supervisee has formed with his client. You should attempt to decipher, consequently, whether your supervisee can understand his client and whether he can comprehend the therapeutic relationship which has been formed.

Practice methodology

Your main focus initially will be to understand the professional practice which your supervisee will conduct. You will, therefore, be required to comprehend the therapeutic methodology and the treatment strategies which your supervisee would normally employ.

You should perceive your supervisee's overall approach to his client and appreciate the extent to which he will truly be proactive and interventionist in assisting him.

Supervisee's professional status

You would be advised to evaluate the extent of your supervisee's experience as a practitioner and his previous experience, if any, of clinical supervision.

The extent of your supervisee's professional practice experience will frequently dictate the nature of his supervisory process with you. You will need to discover, therefore, whether your supervisee is newly qualified and perhaps may be a nervous fledgling or whether he has a wealth of experience on which he can draw. Your supervisee may, moreover, feel very confident when helping others or he may feel rather overwhelmed by his responsibilities. A newly qualified supervisee may require much in the way of hand-holding and mentoring while the more experienced practitioner may only need minimal guidance when he encounters a specific difficulty.

When meeting your supervisee initially you might wish to enquire about his previous experience of the supervisory process in order to ensure that you can meet his professional needs. Your supervisee, for instance, may be thoroughly familiar with the supervisory process but you must iron out any unrealistic expectations or erroneous misconceptions which he may harbour about your supervisory role. If your supervisee is newly qualified you should also enquire about his expectations and his requirements during your supervisory intervention.

CLIENT'S PSYCHOLOGICAL STATUS

You will need to gather as much information as possible about your supervisee's client. From this information-base you can then assist your supervisee to employ his therapeutic techniques and his methodology appropriately with his client.

You will usually need to gather some information about your supervisee's client so that you can understand his therapeutic needs. You may wish to enquire, therefore, about the symptomatic patterns and the psychological health issues of your supervisee's client so that you can comprehend the options available to your supervisee for providing therapeutic assistance.

You should essentially attempt to gauge the degree of therapeutic compliance to which your supervisee's client will adhere. It may be vitally important for your supervisee to comprehend whether or not his client is compliant with the therapeutic process. Your supervisee, for instance, may be beating himself up about his own perceived working failure when actually his client will be the culprit in not moving forward during his therapeutic encounter.

You might want to ask your supervisee about the nature of his client's personal circumstances and whether any unsatisfactory relationships will be significantly impinging on his emotive health and his ability to resolve his symptomatic patterns in the therapeutic context. You may also wish to ask your supervisee about his client's current lifestyle, his occupation, his financial position and his life purpose if these factors are at all relevant to your supervisory intervention. It might also be politic for you to enquire whether your supervisee's client might be seeking any other form of alternative therapeutic assistance.

Finally you may wish to comprehend where your supervisee's client might be coming from in terms of his degree of self-awareness and his personal insight as these factors will often dictate his final therapeutic outcome.

SUPERVISORY ENQUIRY ASSIGNMENT

Answer the questions shown below about supervisory enquiry, pose any further questions which might arise during this process and decide what action, if any, you propose to take as a result of your findings.

- Why will it be necessary for you to undertake a preliminary enquiry and an initial assessment of your supervisee?

- Can you get to grips with appreciating your supervisee both as an individual and as a working professional?

- Do you believe that you fully understand your supervisee and his working methodology?

- What have you concluded about your supervisee's approach to working with his client?

- Does your supervisee lack confidence in his ability as a working professional?

- Can you decipher whether your supervisee's client has a limited self-awareness or a lack of personal insight and whether he is generally compliant with his practitioner and with the therapeutic process?

- What form of distress has your supervisee's client suffered from in terms of his past stressful-traumatic manifestation and his present life-stress dilemma?

- In what ways does your supervisee's client engage in healthy intimate and social relationships?

- Does your supervisee's client possess a debased self-esteem or a poor self-image?

- Is your supervisee's client content with his life's work and has he yet discovered his life-purpose?

Supervisory Guidance

Supervisory guidance principles

When you provide professional guidance for your supervisee you will be dealing essentially with his immediate needs for assistance with his work.

Your role as a supervisor will largely be concerned with assisting your supervisee to function efficiently as a therapeutic practitioner. The supervisory process, therefore, should principally address your supervisee's professional and personal needs in the most effective manner.

Your professional guidance task may be one of gently supporting, steering and mentoring your supervisee in order to allow him to blossom as a practitioner by enhancing his professional competence and by boosting his self-confidence. Your work of supporting, developing and championing your supervisee, therefore, will often be a major factor in the supervisory equation.

At all times you will need to understand and to adapt to your supervisee's unique professional style of working and then offer supervisory guidance within these parameters.

Supportive guidance

You should aim to create a supervisory environment which will provide a confidential and non-judgemental space wherein your supervisee can share his innermost emotive responses, speak honestly about his practice doubts and undertake professional problem-solving in relation to his work.

Your brief will generally be to encourage and to nurture your supervisee as an evolving professional. Your supervisee will have undertaken his training programme and he may have gained experience – however limited – of working practice but he will still need to be matured as a working professional in such a way that he can derive fulfilment and satisfaction from his work. Taking an encouraging stance and constantly championing your supervisee should, therefore, become the order of the day for you.

During the supervisory process you will probably need to assist your supervisee in order to address a number of his personal issues. Should you feel that your supervisee has a number of personal dilemmas which might need to be urgently addressed then you might also wish to steer him in the direction of undertaking further personal therapeutic intervention as necessary.

The personal support element of your supervisory role will, consequently, be akin to the therapeutic function.

MENTORING GUIDANCE

Professional mentoring may entail a degree of problem-solving for your supervisee who will need to find a practical solution to his working dilemmas.

Frequently the supervisory process will be one in which you can promote self-reflection in your supervisee so that he can tap into his inner wisdom as your means of encouraging him to undertake his own problem-solving.

When undertaking practical problem-solving it will usually be advisable for you to expose your supervisee to various therapeutic options which he could undertake with his client rather than making any direct suggestions. Your supervisee, consequently, will be able to select the most appropriate therapeutic techniques from the options available to him for use with his client. By facilitating this form of on-the-job learning you will be expanding your supervisee's repertoire of therapeutic methodology and, simultaneously, you will be providing him with a viable solution.

Often a problem-solving exercise can include a brainstorming session with your supervisee in order to help him to unravel his practice difficulty. You will usually be able to adopt a questioning-and-challenging procedure in order to assist your supervisee with brainstorming so that a workable solution to his practice dilemma can be found.

You may also wish to provide a quality-control facility for your supervisee if you believe that he might be falling short of the mark or, alternatively, if he feels that his skills are in any way inadequate.

Your mentoring role as a supervisor will, consequently, be akin to the training function when assisting your supervisee in this way.

INSPIRATIONAL GUIDANCE

Your supervisee may well be looking to you for inspiration, encouragement and verification that his therapeutic approach and methodology are appropriate for his client.

You will need, therefore, to inspire your supervisee in order to bring out the best in him. Professional inspiration will be a means of spurring your supervisee on and thus ensuring that he does not lack any enthusiasm for his work.

You should also provide your supervisee with verification that his work is being undertaken satisfactorily and that any unfounded self-doubts can be allayed. You may find that you will frequently need to reassure your supervisee about the work which he will be undertaking. Reassurance can be a form of verification that your supervisee is progressing along the right lines with his client. If your supervisee is beset by self-doubt then often a degree of inspirational encouragement and professional validation from you will frequently overcome his practice impasse.

Developmental guidance

You should be able to assist your supervisee with the enhancement of his career as part of your supervisory function. Your work as a supervisor will demand that you can provide a conducive environment for your supervisee so that his work can be enhanced and developed.

You should aim to assist your supervisee with his working practice in order to maximize his professional potential. Your role will thus be one of nurturing your supervisee's professional development, enhancing his professional practice and, perhaps, steering him towards a chosen specialism.

By promoting your supervisee's self-development programme you will, of course, also be enhancing and expanding his professional practice as a consequence. Your supervisee, for instance, will be able to take on more clients once he feels confident in his ability. When discussing a particular case which your supervisee has hitherto not been able to handle, moreover, you will enable him to extend the scope of his working practice.

If it becomes apparent, however, that your supervisee requires a little more than merely on-the-job guidance then it may be appropriate for him to seek further training in the form of a continuing professional development course.

SUPERVISORY GUIDANCE ASSIGNMENT

Answer the questions shown below about supervisory guidance, pose any further questions which might arise during this process and decide what action, if any, you propose to take as a result of your findings.

- What will supervisory guidance for your supervisee entail?
- In what ways might you offer personal and professional support to your supervisee?
- How do you see your role as a supervisor when offering professional guidance to your supervisee?
- Will you be able to hone your mentoring skills in some way in order to assist your supervisee?
- In what way might you undertake a problem-solving exercise with your supervisee?

- Can you encourage your supervisee to expand his repertoire of therapeutic techniques?
- Are you able to validate the work of your supervisee and to inspire him accordingly?
- Will you be able to challenge your supervisee when you believe he might need to be stretched in order to progress?
- Can you allay any of your supervisee's unfounded self-doubts or his practice reservations?
- In what ways could you enhance the practice work of your supervisee and thereby oversee his professional development?

Practice Methodology

Practice Methodology Principles

You will need to appreciate the therapeutic principles which underpin the main psychotherapeutic practices in order to be able to assist a number of hypnotherapy practitioners from varying disciplines who might seek supervisory assistance (see Figure 29: *Practice Methodology*).

Your knowledge of the various therapeutic disciplines will help you to understand the therapeutic angle which your supervisee will be taking with his client. Your supervisee's chosen therapeutic methodology will usually be influenced by his personal preference and his former training.

Questioning in this area will highlight the precise way in which your supervisee will approach and can assist his client. Once you can appreciate the practice principles which your supervisee will employ with his client you will be well placed in order to understand him both as a practitioner and as an individual.

You might be advised, therefore, to acquaint yourself with psychodynamic, humanistic, state-oriented, transpersonal, biodynamic, cognitive and behavioural disciplines within the hypnotherapy-psychotherapy arena in order to understand your supervisee's specific working methodology.

Your supervisee may often, in reality, employ a combination of different practice methodologies and, consequently, you should have a working acquaintance of the complete spectrum of hypnotherapeutic disciplines.

When your supervisee practices a therapeutic discipline which embraces cause-resolution, for instance, he may incorporate psychodynamic, humanistic, state-oriented, transpersonal and biodynamic methodology into his practice.

When your supervisee assists his client to find a solution to his symptomatic patterning, on the other hand, then he will usually employ cognitive and behavioural techniques.

Your knowledge of practice methodology will also be of assistance to you if you intend to work in a supervisory capacity with an alternative practitioner who operates outside the hypnotherapy field.

Figure 29: Practice Methodology

Methodology	Client Focus	Supervisee Focus
Psychodynamic	Client resolves the originating cause of his emotive distress and his relationship disharmony	Symptomatic causes
Humanist	Client optimizes his growth potential and his self-actualization	Symptomatic causes
State-oriented	Client resolves his mind compartmentalization and his memory fragmentation	Symptomatic causes
Transpersonal	Client evolves spiritually according to metaphysical doctrine	Symptomatic causes
Biodynamic	Client addresses the originating cause of his psychosomatic-psychogenic disorder	Symptomatic causes
Cognitive	Client alters his erroneous perception and his faulty cognition	Symptomatic effects
Behavioural	Client overcomes his unhelpful conditioning and his uncontrollable behavioural traits	Symptomatic effects

Psychodynamic methodology

The practitioner of psychodynamic therapy will focus on investigating and resolving the originating cause of his client's emotive dilemma and his relationship disharmony both with others and with himself.

The psychodynamic practitioner will consider the way in which his client will be driven by his unconscious motivation so that root-cause analysis can lead to the resolution of his symptomatic patterning. Psychodynamic practice methodology will, therefore, be an insight-orientated discipline which will aim to achieve psychological balance and harmony for your supervisee's client.

When your supervisee specializes in a psychodynamic practice he will mainly employ therapeutic techniques for age-regression, free association of ideas, symbolic imagery analysis, transference exploration and inner child healing.

Humanistic methodology

The practitioner of humanistic therapy will focus on the psychological growth potential and the self-actualization of his client by utilizing a client-centred approach.

The humanistic practitioner, consequently, will consider ways in which his client can achieve self-fulfilment, can attain his lifetime goals and can work towards harmony within his immediate social environment. If your supervisee practices humanistic therapy he will be forward-looking in his approach to his work with his client but he will also invite him to look back into the past should there be any unfinished business lurking which might inhibit his forward propulsion.

When your supervisee specializes in a humanistic practice he will mainly employ therapeutic techniques for age-regression, age-progression, free association of ideas, transference exploration, therapeutic re-enactment, existential philosophy and inner child healing.

STATE-ORIENTED METHODOLOGY

The practitioner of state-oriented therapy will help his client to resolve any unsatisfactory states of mind which he might exhibit uncontrollably.

The state-oriented practitioner will adhere to the doctrine that his client will be subject to altered states of consciousness, mind compartmentalisation and memory-fragmentation as a result of his stressful-traumatic dilemma. The state-oriented practitioner will frequently utilize the hypnotic state as a means of accessing his client's unhelpful altered states of mind and any preverbal states in which conflict may reside.

When your supervisee specializes in a state-oriented practice he will mainly employ therapeutic techniques for ego-state resolution, ego-strengthening, age-regression, state transcendence, parts therapy and neurolinguistic programming.

Transpersonal methodology

The practitioner of transpersonal therapy will subscribe to metaphysical doctrine which will affirm that his client will reincarnate through a number of lifetimes in order to rid himself of negative karma.

The transpersonal practitioner will thus assist his client to realize his life purpose, to fulfil his true potential and to transcend the earthly plane in his quest for spiritual enlightenment and soul-centred evolution. The transpersonal practitioner, consequently, will be conversant with the concept of reincarnation, karmic resolution, psycho-spiritual exploration, psychosynthesis and metaphysical law.

When your supervisee specializes in a transpersonal practice he will mainly employ therapeutic techniques for spiritual healing, soul-retrieval, spiritual exploration, past-life regression, astral travel and shamanic journeying.

Biodynamic methodology

The practitioner of biodynamic therapy will work with his client's energetic disturbance and his cellular memory with a view to resolving any functional disturbance from a holistic angle.

The biodynamic practitioner will consider that his client's physiological malaise will be a direct result of his psychological stressful-traumatic dilemma. The biodynamic practitioner, therefore, will adhere to the doctrine that his client will be driven by his biological needs and his instinctive drives. The practitioner of biodynamic therapy will also be keenly interested in analysing his client's bodily postures and his body-language.

The biodynamic practitioner will frequently integrate physical contact and spiritual healing techniques into his practice methodology. The biodynamic discipline could also include, for example, the practitioner of homeopathy, nutritional medicine or herbal medicine whom you might also be able to assist in a supervisory capacity.

When your supervisee specializes in a biodynamic practice he will mainly employ therapeutic techniques for body-oriented psychotherapy, energetic healing, psychosomatic-psychogenic resolution and mind-body disharmony healing.

Cognitive methodology

The practitioner of cognitive therapy will help his client to reflect on his erroneous perception, to alter his irrational thinking patterns and to examine the ways in which he lives according to his own set of faulty cognitive schemata.

The cognitive practitioner will mainly aim to help his client to challenge his irrational thinking patterns, to restructure his belief systems and to alter his faulty perception of circumstances so that he can function unhampered in the social world. The cognitive practitioner will also empower his client to achieve his personal goals.

When your supervisee specializes in a cognitive practice he will mainly employ therapeutic techniques for relaxation, belief restructuring, positive thinking, ego-strengthening, assertiveness training, contextual reframing, life-coaching and goal-attainment.

BEHAVIOURAL METHODOLOGY

The practitioner of behavioural therapy will help his client to undertake behavioural analysis with a view to motivating him towards successful goal-attainment and peace of mind.

The behavioural practitioner will consider that his client has been erroneously conditioned to behave in unhelpful ways and that he has lost control of his immediate environment.

When your supervisee specializes in a behavioural practice he will mainly employ therapeutic techniques for motivational task-accomplishment, role-modelling, circumstantial control, faulty-conditioning resolution, desensitization, aversion therapy, ego-strengthening and life-coaching.

Practice methodology assignment

Answer the questions shown below about practice methodology, pose any further questions which might arise during this process and decide what action, if any, you propose to take as a result of your findings.

- Might your supervisee focus on unearthing his client's psychic stressful-traumatic manifestations in relation to his past experiences?

- Will your supervisee be concerned with his client's maturation and self-fulfilment as a means of gaining personal insight and enhancing his self-concept?

- Does your supervisee practice any form of state-oriented psychotherapy by investigating his client's ego-state manifestations, his altered states of consciousness and his memory-fragmentation?

- Is your supervisee interested in his client's self-fulfilment in life and his spiritual transcendence with reference to metaphysical law?

- Might your supervisee utilize practice methodology for healing his client's physiological malaise?

- Would your supervisee be inclined towards clearing his client's energetic biosphere or working with his cellular memory?

- Might your supervisee focus on providing his client with practical tools which will aim to reintegrate him into his social world?

- Could your supervisee challenge his client's irrational thinking patterns and his belief structures as a means of therapeutic assistance?

- Might your supervisee analyse his client's actions in order to formulate a strategy for him to overcome his perceived lack of motivation, his lack of control and his negative conditioning?

- Does your supervisee practice any other form of alternative therapy with his client for which you could offer him supervisory support?

Practice Approach

Practice approach principles

You will need to have an appreciation of your supervisee's preferences in terms of therapeutic treatment strategies and techniques as well as the therapeutic premise from which he will work.

You should, as a matter of course, gauge whether your supervisee will seek to resolve the originating cause of his client's dilemma or whether he will focus on dealing with the symptomatic patterning of his distress.

You may also need to identify your supervisee's treatment approach in terms of length of treatment and the therapeutic methodology which he will employ with his client. Your supervisee may, of course, utilize a blend of treatment approaches, practice methodology and therapeutic tactics with his client.

With this all-embracing knowledge about your supervisee's practice approach you can then usually gauge the way in which his therapeutic treatment strategy with his client will evolve.

Cause-resolution approach

Your supervisee may be interested in helping his client to access and to resolve the originating cause of his symptomatic patterning. Your supervisee, by this means, will be endeavouring to work with the root-cause of his client's dilemma rather than with his presenting symptomatic patterning.

When your supervisee adopts a causative resolution approach he will usually be a practitioner of psychodynamic, humanistic, state-oriented, transpersonal or biodynamic practice methodology.

Your supervisee would usually offer a medium-term or a long-term therapeutic intervention if he considers that his client will require an appreciable number of sessions in order to address his stressful-traumatic dilemma.

Effect-resolution approach

Your supervisee may tend to favour a solution-focused methodology whereby he will endeavour to resolve his client's symptomatic patterning. Your supervisee, by this means, will work with the effect of his client's dilemma rather than with the originating cause of his presenting symptomatic patterning.

When your supervisee adopts an effect-resolution approach he will usually be a practitioner of cognitive or behavioural practice methodology.

Your supervisee will usually offer short-term therapeutic intervention if he considers that his client would only require a few sessions in order to address his stressful-traumatic dilemma.

EMOTIVE-FOCUS APPROACH

You may wish to identify whether your supervisee will be inclined to help his client by focusing on the emotive impact of his symptomatic patterning rather than on the cognitive aspect of his dilemma in the therapeutic context.

If your supervisee favours a medium-term or a long-term treatment plan as a cause-resolution approach with his client then he may be inclined towards an emotive-focus practice strategy. Your supervisee's emotive-focus approach will endeavour to resolve his client's unhelpful emotive reactions and his uncontrollable motivational responses although some cognitive probing may become a necessity during the course of his therapeutic intervention.

COGNITIVE-FOCUS APPROACH

You may wish to identify whether your supervisee will be inclined to help his client by focusing on the cognitive impact of his symptomatic patterning rather than on the emotive aspect of his dilemma in the therapeutic context.

If your supervisee favours a short-term treatment plan as an effect-resolution approach with his client then he may to inclined towards a cognitive-focus practice strategy. Your supervisee's cognitive-focus approach will strive towards resolving his client's unhelpful thinking processes and his irrational reasoning ability although some emotive probing may become a necessity during the course of his therapeutic intervention.

TREATMENT STRATEGY

It will be essential for you to possess an in-depth and a detailed understanding of the treatment methodology which your supervisee would normally employ with his client.

You might wish to make a comprehensive checklist of the treatment techniques and the practice strategy which your supervisee will constantly draw on so that you can obtain a clear picture of him as a working professional. From this vantage-point you could then help your supervisee to expand his therapeutic repertoire, to highlight a given technique which might be appropriate for a specific client and to further his professional development generally.

You may need to identify initially the way in which your supervisee will employ methodology for hypnotic relaxation and creative visualisation. You may also wish to investigate whether your supervisee utilizes supportive listening and counselling methodology with his client.

If your supervisee is a practitioner of a cause-resolution practice methodology then you may wish to establish his approach to utilizing regression techniques, therapeutic re-enactment and imagery-exploration. You might also desire to investigate whether your supervisee would probe any client-transference manifestation and whether he might engage in any counter-transference exploration for his own benefit.

If your supervisee is a practitioner of effect-resolution practice methodology then you may wish to establish his approach to utilizing strategic planning, problem-solving, coping-strategy design, pattern-interrupt techniques, therapeutic desensitization, aversion methodology, symptom-recontextualization, situational-reframing and assertiveness training.

You will also need to enquire whether your supervisee will be inclined to adopt a largely non-interventionist and a non-directive approach or whether he will prefer an interventionist and a directive strategy when assisting his client.

Frequently when your supervisee is an emotive-focused practitioner he will aim for a non-interventionist and a non-directive therapeutic angle. The cognitively focused practitioner may, conversely, be more interventionist and directive in his approach.

You might, furthermore, wish to understand whether your supervisee will utilize verbal techniques, abstract thinking, intuitive processing or provocative probing with his client.

You would also be advised to discover the various ways in which your supervisee will endeavour to assist his client in order to overcome any unconscious resistance, self-sabotage mechanisms, defensive-strategy ploys and self-protection devices.

If your supervisee promotes any specialism then you may need to brush up your knowledge of this particular working practice so that you can help him to enhance his career path.

Environmental factors

You will usually wish to gain an overall awareness of the way in which your supervisee will conduct his therapeutic practice in terms of the logistic circumstances and the therapeutic environment in which he sees his client.

You may need to ascertain whether your supervisee works in a clinical setting or whether he uses his own home as a practice centre.

You could enquire whether your supervisee will see his client face-to-face or whether he will assist him remotely via internet conferencing.

You would also be advised to gauge whether your supervisee will offer his client sessions on a one-to-one basis or whether he conducts group-therapy sessions.

You might, furthermore, need to discover whether your supervisee sees both adult and child clients.

PRACTICE APPROACH ASSIGNMENT

Answer the questions shown below about practice approach, pose any further questions which might arise during this process and decide what action, if any, you propose to take as a result of your findings.

- Do you fully understand the way in which your supervisee will conduct his practice?
- Does your supervisee normally undertake short-term, medium-term or long-term hypno-psychotherapy with his client?
- Will your supervisee undertake supportive listening and client-centred counselling techniques with his client?
- Does your supervisee focus on his client's past issues or his present dilemma for the duration of his therapeutic journey?
- Does your supervisee endeavour to look for any combination of emotive or cognitive influences with his client in order to address his symptomatic patterning?
- What treatment methodology does your supervisee normally employ with his client?

- Will your supervisee usually undertake strategic planning and problem-solving when assisting his client?

- Does your supervisee tend to employ any combination of verbal techniques, abstract thinking, intuitive processing or provocative probing with his client?

- Does your supervisee normally offer one-to-one therapeutic invention with his client or does he undertake any group-work programmes?

- Does your supervisee normally tend to work face-to-face with his client or does he conduct any remote-contact sessions?

SUPERVISORY PRACTICE

SUPERVISEE-CLIENT INTERACTION

SUPERVISEE-CLIENT INTERACTION PRINCIPLES

The main thrust of the supervisory process will usually require you to understand the established and, indeed, the evolving relationship between your supervisee and his client.

Your supervisory role will be to view the interaction between your supervisee and his client from an impartial distance. You will, therefore, need to take an outsider's overview of supervisee-client interaction while simultaneously championing and assisting your supervisee personally.

Your aim should be to safeguard the welfare of both your supervisee and his client when undertaking the task of reviewing supervisee-client interaction. Should you feel, for instance, that your supervisee is being compromised in any way by his client then you will need to intercede in order to safeguard his welfare, his safety and his peace of mind. You might, by the same token, need to intervene if you feel that your supervisee's client will be open to compromise or exploitation by your supervisee.

An unravelling of supervisee-client interaction may be the key factor which will dictate the outcome of your supervisee's therapeutic intervention with his client. Your supervisee may, therefore, find it beneficial to discuss any difficulties which may arise in supervisee-client interaction with a view to ensuring that a sensitive and a delicate situation can be averted or be resolved successfully.

During the supervisory process you may also wish to question your supervisee about why he thinks his client might have chosen him to be his practitioner. This knowledge may shed further light on supervisee-client interaction so that your supervisee will not become embroiled in any conflict even if it might seem to be only embryonic.

Supervisee perspective

You should question your supervisee about his opinion of the relationship which his client may be forming with him. You will then be able to decipher whether your supervisee may be impeded in his therapeutic work and whether he might be suffering as a result of any added burden during the therapeutic process.

Your supervisee may want to talk about his client's projection manifestations, transference episodes and attachment difficulties during the supervisory process. Your supervisee, for instance, may feel that his client can be over-demanding of his attention, expects him to work miracles, desires to be over-friendly, appears to be stroppy or will be arrogantly dictatorial in his consulting room. Any number of factors which might impinge adversely on an unruffled supervisee-client relationship, therefore, may cause your supervisee some distress which will need to be resolved during his supervisory encounter.

Your supervisee may also need to probe his own counter-projection, counter-transference and counter-attachment issues if these seem to be causing concern. If your supervisee, for instance, feels out of control, overwhelmed, threatened or in any way discomforted by his client's words, actions or manner then this matter will be fodder for supervisory discussion. Your supervisee will, of course, need to deal effectively with any such issues in order to maintain his personal equilibrium and to ensure his professional neutrality with his client.

Your supervisee should blossom and become a more effective practitioner once counter-projection, counter-transference and counter-attachment obstacles have been removed from the equation. The value of such phenomenon to your supervisee will be inestimable not only because of the personal insight which he will gain but also so that the smooth-running of his therapeutic practice can be assured.

CLIENT PERSPECTIVE

You may need to obtain a clear impression of where your supervisee's client might be coming from in order to comprehend the nature and the extent of his symptomatic patterning, his stressful-traumatic manifestation and his psychic dilemma.

When you can gain an overview of your supervisee's client from a distance then it will usually be possible for you to provide an unbiased opinion of where he is, what he might need and where he should be going.

The facts which you will gain about your supervisee's client will then permit you to steer any rocky supervisee-client interaction on to safer soil. This bird's-eye view of supervisee-client interaction will allow you to assess your supervisee's client accurately so that you can guide your supervisee accordingly.

You should remember that client-projection, client-transference and client-attachment issues will arise for the therapeutic benefit of your supervisee's client who will make important and insightful realizations as a result of these phenomena. Such issues, however, will require careful negotiation in order to be brought to a point where your supervisee's client will benefit from his insight.

SUPERVISEE-CLIENT INTERACTION ASSIGNMENT

Answer the questions shown below about supervisee-client interaction, pose any further questions which might arise during this process and decide what action, if any, you propose to take as a result of your findings.

- What factors will you need to take into account when investigating your supervisee's relationship with his client?

- Can you gauge whether supervisee-client interaction has been influenced by any unconscious motivation and any repetitive life-patterning which your supervisee's client may exhibit?

- Has your supervisee's client suffered from any loss of love and feelings of abandonment during his life which might prompt him to demand too much of your supervisee's attention?

- Could your supervisee's client be arrogant and rude to his practitioner so that this situation will then shatter your supervisee's confidence?

- Might your supervisee's client be blatantly and rebelliously thwarting all his practitioner's attempts to assist him?

- Does your supervisee's client exhibit a sound commitment to his task of undertaking his therapeutic journey?

- Is your supervisee's client totally compliant with his practitioner and with his therapeutic process?

- Does your supervisee feel out of personal control or flummoxed when working with his client?

- In what ways might your supervisee be adversely effected by working with his client?

- Do you consider that you would be easily able to spot any client-projection, client-transference or client-attachment manifestation by questioning your supervisee closely?

SUPERVISEE-CLIENT PHENOMENA

SUPERVISEE-CLIENT PHENOMENA PRINCIPLES

It may be helpful for you to understand the various forms of supervisee-client phenomena which include client-projection, client-transference and client-attachment as well as the manifestations of counter-projection, counter-transference and counter-attachment issues which your supervisee may experience in the course of his work (see Figure 30: *Supervisee-Client Phenomena*).

When your supervisee is faced with having to handle problematic supervisee-client interaction issues there will be a need for him to remain unruffled, empathetic and neutral in his dealings with his client in order to successfully reap the therapeutic benefit of such phenomena.

When you can help your supervisee to identify any forms client-projection, client-transference and client-attachment which has manifested in his client then this knowledge will go a long way towards assisting him in his working practice.

Counter-projection, counter-transference and counter-attachment issues will almost inevitably arise as a natural phenomenon during professional practice but your supervisee should be sensitively assisted to appreciate the significance of such a manifestation and to resolve it decisively.

FIGURE 30: SUPERVISEE-CLIENT PHENOMENA

PHENOMENA	CLIENT FOCUS	SUPERVISEE FOCUS
Projection	Client unconsciously believes that his practitioner possesses his own unacknowledged character traits	Practitioner unconsciously believes that his client possesses his own unacknowledged character traits
Transference	Client unconsciously views his practitioner as if he were a problem-person from his own life	Practitioner unconsciously views his client as if he were a problem-person from his own life
Attachment	Client unconsciously seeks to rely on his practitioner as if he were a parent	Practitioner unconsciously seeks to rely on his client as if he were a parent

CLIENT-PROJECTION

The phenomenon of client-projection will manifest when your supervisee's client unconsciously imagines that his practitioner possesses certain character traits which actually emanate from his own unconscious mind because these qualities are as yet unacknowledged.

Client-projection will arise when your supervisee's client does not wish to acknowledge his own perceived shortcomings, his limitations or his praiseworthy qualities. Your supervisee's client, for instance, may be heartily ashamed to admit to certain socially unacceptable character traits and he may even accuse his practitioner of exhibiting traits which are considered to be wicked or distasteful.

Your supervisee's client, conversely, may also fail to acknowledge his own praiseworthy personal qualities because of his debased self-esteem. Your supervisee's client could, for instance, be reluctant to acknowledge his intelligence or his notable accomplishments but he might envisage such qualities in his practitioner.

CLIENT-TRANSFERENCE

The phenomenon of client-transference will arise when your supervisee's client unconsciously imagines that his practitioner possesses certain qualities or exhibits specific behaviours which remind him of another problem-person in his life (see Figure 31: *CLIENT-TRANSFERENCE*).

Client-transference will often occur when your supervisee's client cannot consciously acknowledge the fact that another person has caused him inner conflict and unwarranted distress. Your supervisee's client could, for instance, be unable to acknowledge the wrongdoings of a parent, a close relative or other childhood carer.

Your supervisee's client may, alternatively, be reluctant to acknowledge the way in which he is being currently ill-treated by an intimate partner or by a close friend.

Client-transference phenomena can be classified as either a positive phenomenon or a negative phenomenon which your supervisee's client will exhibit according to whether the transference manifestation can be regarded as either socially acceptable or socially unacceptable.

FIGURE 31: CLIENT-TRANSFERENCE

TRANSFERENCE	CLIENT FOCUS	CLASSIFICATION
Object	Client regards his practitioner as an object for his personal need-satisfaction	Positive
Rewarding	Client feels able to derive personal benefit from his practitioner	Positive
Legitimate	Client regards his practitioner as a knowledgeable and an authoritative person	Positive
Expert	Client regards his practitioner as a qualified and a skilled professional	Positive

Referred	Client regards his practitioner as an interesting and an amiable person	Positive
Coercive	Client feels controlled and manipulated by his practitioner	Negative
Erotic	Client feels love and sexual attraction for his practitioner	Negative
Idealising	Client regards his practitioner as a heroic person	Negative
Illusional	Client regards his practitioner as a godlike person	Negative
Delusional	Client believes his practitioner to be superhuman	Negative

CLIENT-ATTACHMENT

You should be aware that your supervisee's client may become overly reliant on his practitioner and this situation may become a subject for supervisory discussion when a too-close-for-comfort client-attachment has manifested (see Figure 32: *CLIENT-ATTACHMENT*).

Your supervisee's client may unconsciously form an insecure attachment to his practitioner particularly if he felt unloved, ill-treated or abandoned in his childhood. If your supervisee's client, for instance, felt bereft early in life then he may have developed an unhealthy need to over-depend on others. Your supervisee may, therefore, become the life-raft to which his client may obsessively cling in desperation.

Client-attachment phenomena can be classified as either an anxiety-provoking attachment or a motivational attachment according to whether your supervisee's client will be driven by his emotive responses or by his physical action.

FIGURE 32: CLIENT-ATTACHMENT

ATTACHMENT	CLIENT FOCUS	CLASSIFICATION
Anxious	Client becomes anxious to please his practitioner	Anxiety-provoking
Anxious-resistant	Client resists separation from his practitioner	Anxiety-provoking
Anxious-avoidant	Client resists help from his practitioner	Anxiety-provoking
Self-reliant	Client becomes compulsively independent of his practitioner	Motivational
Care-giving	Client becomes a compulsive helper of his practitioner	Motivational
Disorganized-disoriented	Client becomes confused by his practitioner	Motivational

Supervisee counter-projection

The phenomenon of counter-projection will arise when your supervisee unconsciously imagines that his own unacknowledged character traits are evident in his client.

Your supervisee, therefore, may not wish to acknowledge his own exemplary qualities or he may seek to suppress his supposedly undesirable character traits and his motivations but he may unconsciously believe that his client exhibits such qualities.

Issues of professional uncertainty or personal self-doubt may often need to be explored in the supervisory context when your supervisee exhibits counter-projection phenomena. Your supervisee might, for instance, be beset by a sense of worthlessness and he may exhibit a negative false perception of his own ability but he may then believe his client to be hugely powerful.

Supervisee counter-transference

The phenomenon of counter-transference will arise when your supervisee imagines that his client possesses qualities or adopts behaviours which remind him of another problem-person in his life.

A counter-transference manifestation may take the form of an emotive response, a human character trait or a behavioural stance from your supervisee. Should you perceive any manifestation of counter-transference – particularly any negative form – then your role will be to gently encourage your supervisee to gain enlightenment and therapeutic resolution so that he can flourish personally and develop professionally.

Supervisee counter-transference will often occur when your supervisee, for instance, becomes aware of the fact that his client has caused him some inner conflict and this insight should prompt him to discuss the situation in the supervisory context. It may also be that you will detect the manifestation of counter-transference within your supervisee and you should then sensitively broach the subject in order to bring about his own healing resolution and thereby assist him in his professional work.

Supervisee counter-transference phenomena can be classified as either a positive phenomenon or a negative phenomenon which your supervisee will undergo according to whether the counter-transference manifestation can be regarded as either socially acceptable or sociably unacceptable.

Your supervisee will usually be consciously aware of his positive counter-transference manifestation and he should then be able to maintain neutrality and empathy when assisting his client. Your supervisee, therefore, will be able to attune to his client's psyche in order to value and to respect him.

Your supervisee will usually not be overtly aware of his negative counter-transference manifestation because the therapeutic setting will have unconsciously activated his personal issues and, perhaps, may have blurred the boundaries of ethical supervisee-client interaction. Your supervisee could seek to engage his client in some way and then expect him to respond accordingly when negative counter-transference arises. Your supervisee's client may, in these circumstance, feel compromised and so this situation ought to be avoided at all costs.

Your supervisee, for instance, may feel over-anxious about his client's perceived degree of therapeutic success and he will, therefore, seek personal admiration from him. Your supervisee might, similarly, become patronizing, exploitative or over-curious about his client.

Issues of professional uncertainty or personal self-doubt may often need to be explored in the supervisory context by your supervisee who might exhibit counter-transference phenomena.

Your supervisee might, for instance, be beset by a lack of professional confidence or a fear of failure because he might never have received praise from his parents or his childhood efforts were dismissed by a teacher. Your supervisee may then seek validation from his client as a means of supposedly comforting himself.

SUPERVISEE COUNTER-ATTACHMENT

Your supervisee may unconsciously form an insecure anxiety-provoking or a motivational attachment to his client particularly if he felt unloved, ill-treated or abandoned in his childhood.

Should you detect any signs of unwanted attachment in your supervisee then your function will be to help him to understand and to overcome such inclinations as your means of allowing him to work within ethical boundaries with his client.

Your supervisee may, for instance, wish to rely heavily on his client or to feel a strong kinship towards him in order to feel safe at an unconscious level.

SUPERVISEE-CLIENT PHENOMENA ASSIGNMENT

Answer the questions shown below about supervisee-client phenomena, pose any further questions which might arise during this process and decide what action, if any, you propose to take as a result of your findings.

- Why will it be important for you to understand supervisee-client phenomena?
- Do you believe that some form of positive transference manifestation could be oiling the wheels of the therapeutic encounter between your supervisee and his client?

- Is your supervisee empathetic, neutral and non-judgemental at all times with his client?
- Does your supervisee naturally complement his client's psyche in order to assist him with his therapeutic journey?
- Has your supervisee's client developed any form of psychological attachment to your supervisee?
- Does your supervisee tend to act in any way which might not be conducive to his client's therapeutic benefit?
- Does your supervisee tend to become overly anxious about his client's progress or the outcome of his therapeutic journey?
- Does your supervisee tend to judge his own level of professional competence in terms of his client's performance in the therapeutic context?
- Does your supervisee endeavour to seek admiration or validation from his client?
- Does your supervisee in any way tend to exploit his client, to patronize him or to act inappropriately?

SUPERVISORY STYLE

SUPERVISORY STYLE PRINCIPLES

The supervisory style which you might adopt in your practice may vary according to your supervisee's preferred treatment methodology, his practice approach, his individual psyche and his background experience (see Figure 36: *SUPERVISORY STYLE*).

Supervisory styles may, of course, differ widely in terms of the focus of your supervisory interaction with your supervisee and, indeed, you may wish to employ a combination of styles in order to cater for his needs.

You might need to consider your supervisor-supervisee relationship in terms of whether you principally intend to focus on assisting your supervisee personally or else helping him professionally. Ideally, of course, you should aim to assist your supervisee in any way which will be appropriate for his needs and this supervisory route will frequently involve a blend of different styles.

Figure 36: Supervisory Style

Style	Supervisory Focus
Formative	Supervisee focuses on his professional learning and development
Restorative	Supervisee focuses on his therapeutic interaction with his client
Collegiate	Supervisor adopts a master-master relationship with his supervisee
Authoritative	Supervisor adopts a master-apprentice relationship with his supervisee

Formative style

You can utilize a formative supervisory style when you seek to augment your supervisee's existing training foundation in order to develop his career as a working professional.

When your supervisory approach focuses on your supervisee's career development during his supervisory process you will be encouraging him to enhance his previous learning experience. You should, therefore, be familiar with the training programme which your supervisee has already undertaken. With the formative approach to supervision you may, indeed, have previously taught your supervisee on his initial practitioner training course.

The formative supervisory style will, consequently, be akin to the training function and, therefore, you should be conversant with both training techniques and therapeutic procedures in order to assist your supervisee.

Restorative style

You can utilize a restorative supervisory style when your supervisee encounters significant emotive distress as a result of his interaction with his client.

When your supervisee needs to access and to resolve a highly disturbing practice dilemma which has appreciably affected him then a restorative supervisory style will usually be the most appropriate. You may, therefore, need to be familiar with a number of therapeutic practice techniques from an eclectic standpoint in order to assist your supervisee.

The restorative supervisory style will, consequently, be akin to therapeutic intervention and, therefore, you should be able to select some practice methodology which will be appropriate for your supervisee.

Collegiate style

You may wish to utilize a collegiate style of supervisory intervention with your supervisee by considering both parties in the supervisory equation as equal participants.

With a collegiate style of supervision you will, therefore, be addressing your supervisee as a colleague of equal standing to yourself as if you were offering guidance to a fellow-practitioner. With the collegiate supervisory style you should regard yourself as a master discussing matters with another master.

The master-to-master style of supervision can be most appropriate, for instance, when your supervisee is an experienced practitioner who might simply need to consult you for a second opinion with minimal supervisory guidance on your part.

Authoritative style

You may wish to utilize an authoritative style of supervisory intervention if your supervisee is a relative newcomer to the profession and, therefore, he wishes to consult a higher authority when practice difficulties arise.

The master-apprentice style will be most appropriate, for instance, if your supervisee is newly qualified and, therefore, he lacks professional experience. If your supervisee is a newcomer to the profession he may need to look up to you as one who can offer guidance because of your extensive experience of working in the profession.

Supervisory strategy

Once you have adopted a viable supervisory style with your supervisee you can then select some appropriate methodology for use during his supervisory sessions.

When assisting a hypnotherapy practitioner it will usually be most appropriate for you to utilize some imaginative methodology in order to facilitate his personal development and his career progression.

You can usually make judicious use, therefore, of metaphorical imaginary, inner child methodology, ego-state practice, therapeutic re-enactment and art therapy techniques with your supervisee.

You could, for instance, invite your supervisee to imaginatively re-enact his therapeutic sessions with his client in order to see whether a different outcome would be feasible or perhaps be more productive.

You might similarly encourage your supervisee to utilize a dissociative technique whereby he can view his supervisee-client interaction from a safe distance and then offer himself some guidance by becoming his own inner adviser.

You could equally invite your supervisee to imagine what it would be like to become his own client in order to allow him to visualize the therapeutic process from his client's perspective.

It may also be prudent for you to encourage your supervisee to undertake some form of inner child therapeutic rescue as a restorative facility on occasion.

SUPERVISORY STYLE ASSIGNMENT

Answer the questions shown below about supervisory style, pose any further questions which might arise during this process and decide what action, if any, you propose to take as a result of your findings.

- Do you fully appreciate the need to adopt a directional focus in your sessions with your supervisee?

- When might you wish to adopt a formative style with your trainee and in what ways could your supervisory sessions be akin to training?

- Is your supervisee an uncertain fledgling practitioner who might be struggling with the world of working as a hypnotherapy professional?

- When might it be appropriate for you to adopt a restorative supervisory style with your supervisee and in what ways could your supervisory sessions be akin to therapeutic intervention?

- Is your supervisee an experienced professional who might be suffering from the rigours of working with a difficult client?

- When might it be most appropriate for you to employ a collegiate style with your supervisee?

- Do you see yourself in a master-master relationship with your supervisee and will this style be ideal for his needs?

- Do you consider yourself to be in a master-apprentice relationship with your supervisee and will this style be appropriate for his requirements?

- Have you formulated a number of supervisory strategies which you could employ when working with your supervisee?

- Have you considered utilizing supervisory techniques which combine metaphorical imagery, inner child methodology, ego-state therapy, therapeutic re-enactment, art therapy or dissociative techniques with your supervisee?

SUPERVISORY APPROACH

SUPERVISORY APPROACH PRINCIPLES

Established approaches to supervision may take the form of a phased strategy for working with your supervisee and conducting the supervisory process in a number of prescribed stages (see Figure 33: SUPERVISORY APPROACH).

The most common forms of the phased supervisory approach are the three-phase supervisory approach and the seven-phase supervisory approach both of which can provide the framework for your proposed interaction with your supervisee.

The broad-brush stages of the supervisory procedure may transit a number of phrases from an initial needs-assessment before a plan of action can be formulated and put into practice. These supervisory stages will usually begin with an identification of your supervisee's practice difficulty which you can then document and discuss as necessary.

You and your supervisee will next formulate an action-plan which he can put into practice in his workplace. Your supervisee will subsequently decide whether his action-plan will be workable or whether any modifications may need to be made in the light of events in order to ensure a satisfactory resolution of his practice impasse.

FIGURE 33: SUPERVISORY APPROACH

PHASE	SUPERVISORY FOCUS
Evaluate practice dilemma	Supervisee outlines his practice dilemma
Monitor practice dilemma	Supervisee gathers facts
Plan remedial action	Supervisee formulates his action-plan
Expedite remedial action	Supervisee puts his action-plan into practice
Monitor remedial action	Supervisee evaluates the results of his action-plan
Expedite remedial action modification	Supervisee adjusts his action-plan as necessary

THREE-PHASE APPROACH

The three-phase supervisory approach will call for a self-reflective response from your supervisee in order to solve his practice dilemma during the action-planning stage of the supervisory process (see Figure 34: *THREE-PHASE SUPERVISORY APPROACH*).

The three-phase approach to supervision will require you to undertake a degree of information-gathering about your supervisee's practice dilemma before encouraging him to reflect on this predicament. This reflective period can then allow you to facilitate some form of therapeutic investigation with a view to helping your supervisee to resolve his difficulty by gaining personal insight. Your supervisee should now be equipped to formulate a remedy for his practice dilemma. Your supervisee will have thus acquired the tools in order to overcome his practice dilemma with his new-found insight and personal understanding.

The three-phase supervisory approach can be used with your supervisee for any reasonably straightforward practice dilemma and will constitute a general rule-of-thumb format which you can adopt as the norm. Your supervisee, furthermore, can benefit personally from the three-phase approach because of the therapeutic value of his self-reflective strategy.

FIGURE 34: THREE-PHASE SUPERVISORY APPROACH

PHASE	SUPERVISORY FOCUS
Fact-gathering	Supervisor questions his supervisee about his practice dilemma
Reflection-response	Supervisor facilitates psychotherapeutic investigation into his supervisee's practice dilemma
Action	Supervisee gains insight into his practice dilemma and takes remedial action

SEVEN-PHASE APPROACH

The seven-phase supervisory approach will consider supervisee-client interaction as the main focus of attention in order solve your supervisee's practice dilemma (see Figure 35: SEVEN-PHASE SUPERVISORY APPROACH).

The seven-phase supervisory approach will begin with an initial information-gathering procedure in order to document your supervisee's practice dilemma and to challenge any erroneous assumptions which he may harbour about his work-based difficulty. You can now outline the possible solution options from which your supervisee can select the most appropriate choice for his purpose.

The seven-phase supervisory approach will also allow for an exploration of client-transference issues and any of your supervisee's counter-transference manifestations.

You may also be able to utilize your own supervisor-supervisee relationship as a model for helping your supervisee to solve his practice dilemma.

You can finally encourage your supervisee to reflect on the outcome of his supervisory encounter and the way in which he could solve his practice predicament as a result of his deliberations and his discoveries. The seven-phase supervisory approach will usually be the most appropriate when your supervisee or his client might be undergoing significant emotive turmoil.

The seven-phase approach to supervision will usually entail a more in-depth analysis of your supervisee's practice impasse and this methodology will usually be able to resolve any knotty problems which supervisee-client interaction may have engendered.

Figure 35: Seven-Phase Supervisory Approach

Phase	Supervisory Focus
Exploration	Supervisee gathers facts about his supervisee's practice dilemma
Investigation	Supervisor enumerates options for solving his supervisee's practice dilemma
Transference	Supervisor facilitates resolution of client-transference issues
Counter-transference	Supervisor facilitates resolution of supervisee counter-transference issues

Supervisor-supervisee relationship	Supervisor and supervisee reflect on the supervisor-supervisee relationship in order to model supervisee-client interaction
Reflection	Supervisee reflects of all facets of the dynamic supervisory process

SUPERVISORY APPROACH ASSIGNMENT

Answer the questions shown below about supervisory approach, pose any further questions which might arise during this process and decide what action, if any, you propose to take as a result of your findings.

- Do you understand the importance of adopting a planned approach to working with your supervisee on his practice dilemma?

- Can you outline the general approach which you might take in order to solve your supervisee's practice predicament?

- What are the features and the advantages of the three-stage supervisory approach?

- How might you adopt the principles of the three-phase supervisory approach in your interaction with your supervisee?

- In what ways could the three-phase supervisory approach apply to your supervisee?

- In what circumstance might you employ the seven-phase supervisory approach with your supervisee?

- What might be the advantage of adopting a supervisory approach in which your supervisee can investigate his own personal dilemmas when working with his client?

- Are you aware that your supervisee can solve his own practice problems with a little encouragement and reflective exploration?

- Do you appreciate that the supervisory encounter will be an organic and a dynamic process?

- Can you see the way in which you could enhance both the professional standing and the personal wellbeing of your supervisee using a phased supervisory approach strategy?

Supervisory Organization

Supervisory organization principles

Supervision may be organized as individual supervisory sessions, as group supervision or as peer-support group supervision.

Your supervisee may require a number of private sessions on a one-to-one basis particularly if his requirements are unique and, therefore, he might warrant some personal attention.

A number of supervisees may be assisted as a group particularly when their training and their level of experience are largely similar. A supervisory group may be formed as a facilitator-lead group or as a peer-support group.

INDIVIDUAL SUPERVISION

You may conduct individual supervision on a one-to-one basis with your supervisee when circumstances dictate.

Your supervisee might elect to undertake individual supervisory sessions because he might have special needs. Your supervisee may, for instance, require regular one-to-one sessions in order to comply with current legislation or with professional body guidelines.

Your supervisee, alternatively, may only call for assistance when he encounters a specific difficult when working with a given client once his clinical practice has been established.

One-to-one supervision will be ideal for the practitioner who is newly qualified who may feel uncertain about his practice methodology and his personal reaction to working with a given client.

GROUP SUPERVISION

Your main task when organizing group supervision will be to ensure that your group runs smoothly and efficiently and that you do not allow any problematic group-dynamics to rule the roost.

A supervisory group can be formed because of your supervisee's inherent need to belong in the social setting in which he can share his thoughts, his feelings and his experiences with other like-minded people in a nurturing environment.

You would be advised to understand each group-participant personally in terms his personality traits and his particular needs in order to ensure that each group-member will receive an equal share of the limelight.

You should, consequently, be on the lookout for any signs of competitiveness or power-struggles between any of your supervisees in order to be able to avert an unpleasant situation when necessary.

You should, moreover, be aware of any attention-seeking ploys by any of your supervisees in case the delicate balance of power within the supervisory group becomes unmanageable. A supervisory group with a negative group-character, or a number of participants who are seeking a scapegoat from within the group, will be a situation which you will want to avoid at all costs.

You should, by the same token, be aware of any group-member who might suffer from a fear of exposure because he may feel disinclined to openly share his views with others or to ask for help while in the group environment.

You may also need to decide whether your supervisory group will consist of homogenous or mixed participants. A supervisory group may be somewhat problematic to facilitate when your participants come from different therapeutic persuasions, have dissimilar backgrounds or have varying levels of experience – although such difficulties are by no means insurmountable.

SUPERVISORY GROUP CONDUCT

The formation of a supervisory group will normally transit a number of stages in order to allow your group to form and to function successfully as a whole unit (see Figure 37: *Supervisory Group Conduct*).

Your supervisory group will firstly need to convene in order to set its overall objectives. Your group must form initially with the agreement of all participants who can establish a workable group-identity. Your group, therefore, should formulate the ground-rules, could elect a facilitator as necessary and then agree the way forward in principle.

Once your group has convened you will need to ensure that some supervisory objectives can be set which will meet the requirements of all participants. You may need to facilitate some form of brain-storming exercise so that ideas can be suggested for the conduct of group sessions and the running of the group. Your group must then find ways of satisfactorily maintaining and, if necessary, modifying its objectives in the interests of all members.

Once your group has been established you will need to monitor its performance in order to ensure that it meets its objectives, that the needs of each participant are fully met and that the group can be viably maintained. Any failure to maintain the group and to facilitate ongoing dynamic action with the full co-operation of each participant may mean that the venture will collapse.

FIGURE 37: SUPERVISORY GROUP CONDUCT

STAGE	SUPERVISORY FOCUS
Formation	Group forms and establishes a group-identity
Formulation	Group identifies needs and sets its objectives
Maintenance	Group maintains its brief and fulfil its objectives
Performance	Group ensures ongoing dynamic action
Adjournment	Group suspends its activity or disbands when necessary

SUPERVISORY GROUP STYLE

You may organize your supervisory group by adopting a number of different supervisory styles which will dictate the way in which your group activity will be conducted (see Figure 38: SUPERVISORY GROUP STYLE).

The main supervisory group styles are authoritative, participative, co-operative and peer-support supervision all of which will call for a different supervisory approach.

An authoritative supervisory group style will require you to become the group-facilitator who will generally organize and will lead the group sessions with participants becoming the receivers rather than being proactive. You might adopt an authoritative group style for a number of newly qualified practitioners who may be inexperienced in organizing supervisory activity.

A participative supervisory group style will encourage participation from all group-members even though you may be the facilitator of the group. A participative group style may be more appropriate for a group of practitioners who have similar needs for assistance and a willingness to openly share ideas and experiences.

A co-operative supervisory group style will have no formal facilitator but each participant will be asked to take the lead as the group-organizer on a rotational basis. The co-operative group style will afford each group-participant an opportunity to manage, to conduct and to steer the supervisory activity in the appropriate direction. The co-operative group style will be most suitable for a number of experienced practitioners who are familiar with the process of supervisory intervention.

A peer-support supervisory group style will not necessarily have a formal group-facilitator but will be organized according to the needs of all participants who can be assisted by their peers.

A peer-support group may be formed for the expressed purpose of gathering a number of like-minded practitioners together regularly in order to undertake joint practice problem-solving.

FIGURE 38: SUPERVISORY GROUP STYLE

STYLE	SUPERVISORY FOCUS
Authoritative	Group-facilitator regards participants as an audience
Participative	Group-facilitator encourages participation from all group-participants
Co-operative	Group-facilitator is appointed on a rotational basis
Peer support	Group-participants undertake joint problem-solving

SUPERVISORY ORGANIZATION ASSIGNMENT

Answer the questions shown below about supervisory organization, pose any further questions which might arise during this process and decide what action, if any, you propose to take as a result of your findings.

- Do you fully appreciate the intrinsic value of ongoing supervision for your supervisee?
- In what ways do you intend to organize your supervisory programme?
- When might individual supervision for your supervisee be more appropriate than group supervision?

- Can you foresee any drawbacks to forming and to running a supervisory group?
- What factors will you bear in mind when inviting participants to join a supervisory group and will you undertake any form of vetting process for new applicants?
- How will you embark on the task of forming and maintaining your supervisory group?
- In what circumstances might you employ an authoritative supervisory style when conducting your group-supervision sessions?
- What might be the value of a participative group supervisory style for your group-participants?
- Can you foresee an occasion when a co-operative supervisory approach would be most appropriate for your supervisory group?
- Would you want to encourage your supervisee to join a peer-support supervisory group?

SUPERVISORY MODELS

SUPERVISION MODELS

A supervision model will be an outline framework which will describe the supervisory process and will outline the strategies which you might employ in order to assist your supervisee (see Figure 39: *SUPERVISORY MODELS*).

Supervisory models can be classified as either psychotherapeutic supervisory models or developmental supervisory models according to whether you might focus on your supervisee's personal practice dilemmas or concentrate on his career development. You may, of course, wish to glean ideas from a number of different models in order to structure your own supervisory sessions with your supervisee in the most appropriate way for his requirements.

The psychotherapeutic supervisory models can be utilized in order to direct your supervisee's attention towards the mechanics of supervisee-client interaction and his personal emotive reactions to the therapeutic encounter.

The developmental supervisory models will focus on your supervisee's career advancement and his professional development.

FIGURE 39: SUPERVISORY MODELS

Model	Supervisory Focus	Classification
Psychodynamic	Supervisee focuses on his psychological issues	Psychotherapeutic
Client-centred	Supervisee focuses on his client's psychological issues	Psychotherapeutic
Supervisee-centred	Supervisee focuses on his practice issues	Psychotherapeutic
Matrix-centred	Supervisee focuses on supervisee-client interaction and supervisor-supervisee interaction	Psychotherapeutic
Person-centred	Supervisee focuses on his self-actualization	Psychotherapeutic
Cognitive-behavioural	Supervisee focuses on his faulty cognition	Psychotherapeutic
Integrated development	Supervisee progresses through entry-level, mid-level and competence-level	Developmental
Tiered development	Supervisee progresses from novice to senior professional	Developmental

Psychodynamic supervision

The psychodynamic model of supervision will consider your supervisee's practice dilemma from the standpoint of his own emotive issues and his counter-transference manifestations as well as facilitating an enquiry into his client's defensive strategies and his transference manifestations.

The psychodynamic model will adhere to the principle of utilizing therapeutic intervention as a means of solving your supervisee's practice dilemma from a psychological perspective.

Client-centred supervision

The client-centred model of supervision will consider your supervisee's practice dilemma from the standpoint of his client's emotive issues and his resistance manifestation.

The client-centred model will probe the world of your supervisee's client from a theoretical perspective rather than focusing on your supervisee's personal issues.

Supervisee-centred supervision

The supervisee-centred model of supervision will consider your supervisee's practice dilemma from the standpoint of his personal difficulties with his work.

The supervisee-centred model will probe the psyche of your supervisee by encouraging self-reflection about his practice methodology rather than focusing on his client's therapeutic issues.

MATRIX-CENTRED SUPERVISION

The matrix-centred model of supervision will analyse supervisee-client interaction by utilizing the supervisor-supervise encounter as a benchmark.

The matrix-centred model will encourage your supervisee to examine the nature of his relationship with his client and to reflect on any similarities between that relationship and the one which he will form with you as his supervisor during the supervisory process.

PERSON-CENTRED SUPERVISION

The person-centred model of supervision will endeavour to assist your supervisee towards self-growth, self-actualization, self-fulfilment and optimization of potential.

The person-centred model will draw heavily on humanistic therapeutic principles in order to allow your supervisee to grow as an individual practitioner.

COGNITIVE-BEHAVIOURAL SUPERVISION

The cognitive-behavioural model of supervision will probe your supervisee's erroneous assumptions and will examine his unhelpful cognitive schemata in connection with his view of his client.

The cognitive-behavioural model will draw heavily on cognitive-behavioural therapeutic principles in order to allow your supervisee to examine his practice dilemma.

INTEGRATED-DEVELOPMENT SUPERVISION

The integrated-development model of supervision will acknowledge your supervisee's level of experience and you should nurture him accordingly.

The integrated-development model will categorize your supervisee as a fledgling practitioner, as a mid-level practitioner or as an experienced professional and his supervisory programme can then be organized accordingly. You should, of course, continually bear in mind the level of experience of your supervisee and adapt your approach to fit his needs.

TIERED-DEVELOPMENT SUPERVISION

The tiered-development model of supervision will favour your supervisee's career enhancement and development which will be seen as consisting of six levels of experience.

Your supervisee will usually be assessed in terms of the number of years which he has been in practice and he will then be allotted a supervisor who will be appropriate to his hierarchical level of experience.

The tiered-development model of supervision will normally be adopted by the mainstream psychotherapist as a means of progressing a new recruit up the professional ladder as his experience grows.

SUPERVISORY MODELS ASSIGNMENT

Answer the questions shown below about supervisory models, pose any further questions which might arise during this process and decide what action, if any, you propose to take as a result of your findings.

- In what ways can your work as a supervisor benefit from your understanding and your insight about supervisory practice models?

- How would you distinguish between a psychotherapeutic model of supervision and a developmental model of supervision?
- Can you encourage your supervisee to consider the emotive impact of his work with his client and could you invite him to undergo some beneficial self-reflection?
- Which of the psychotherapeutic models would be most appropriate for your supervisee?
- Will your supervisory practice focus largely on the needs of your supervisee or on the difficulties of his client?
- In what way might you utilize a matrix-centred model of supervision with your supervisee?
- Can you adapt your supervisory approach to the practice methodology adopted by your supervisee?
- What supervisory methodology would you employ if your supervisee were a newly qualified trainee?
- What supervisory approach would you utilize if your supervisee were an experienced professional?
- What benefit can your supervisee personally derive from receiving supervisory sessions with you?

APPENDICES

FURTHER READING

Ambrose S A et al (2010) *How Learning Works: Seven Research-Based Principles for Smart Teaching*. San Francisco: Jossey-Bass.

Armitage A et al (2007) *Teaching and Training in Post-Compulsory Education*. Buckingham: Open University Press.

Blunt R (1991) *Waldorf Education in Theory and Practice*. Cape Town: Novalis Press.

Cohen L, Mannion L & Morrison K (2004) *A Guide to Teaching Practice*. London: Routledge.

Curzon L B & Tummons J (2013) *Teaching in Further Education: An Outline of Principles and Practice*. London: Bloomsbury Academic.

Eastwood L et al (2009) *A Toolkit for Creative Teaching in Post-Compulsory Education*. Buckingham: Open University Press.

Fawbert F (2008) *Teaching in Post-Compulsory Education: Skills, Standards and Lifelong Learning.* London: Continuum International Publishing Group.

Goodfellow R & Lea M (2013) *Literacy in the Digital University: Critical Perspectives on Learning, Scholarship and Technology Research into Higher Education.* Oxford: Routledge.

Harvey B & Harvey J (2013) *Creative Teaching Approaches in the Lifelong Learning Sector.* Huddersfield: Routledge.

Harwood A C (2013) *The Way of a Child: An Introduction to Steiner Education and the Basics of Child Development.* London: Sophia Books.

Hawkins P & Shohet R (2012) *Supervision in the Helping Professions.* Buckingham: Open University Press.

James U (2015) *Clinical Hypnosis Textbook: A Guide to Practical Intervention.* London: Radcliffe Publishing.

Morison J (2016) *Creative Analytical Hypnotherapy: The Practitioner's Handbook.* Cheltenham: Jacquelyne Morison Publishing.

Morison J (2010) *Analytical Hypnotherapy Volume 1: Theoretical Principles.* Carmarthen: Crown House Publishing.

Morison J (2009) *Analytical Hypnotherapy Volume 2: Practical Applications.* Carmarthen: Crown House Publishing.

Morison J (2008) *The Truly Dynamic Therapist*. Milton Keynes: Author House.

Neary M (2002) *Curriculum Studies in Post-Compulsory and Adult Education: A Teacher's and Student Teacher's Study Guide*. Cheltenham: Nelson Thornes.

Petty G (2009) *Evidence-Based Teaching: A Practical Approach*. Oxford: Oxford University Press.

Petty G (2014) *Teaching Today: A Practical Guide*. Oxford: Oxford University Press.

Reece I & Walker S (2007) *Teaching, Training and Learning: A Practical Guide*. London: Business Education Publishers Ltd.

Rogers A & Horrocks N (2010) *Teaching Adults*. Berkshire: McGraw-Hill Education.

Spalding D (2014) *How To Teach Adults*. San Francisco: Jossey-Bass.

300

INDEX

Active learning process, 88, 90, 145, 148, 165, 167, 169

Active-engagement learning process, 116, 117

Adult learner, 29, 30, 31, 124, 130, 132, 136

Affective learning, 96

Analogical learning, 119

Andragogic learning. See TRAINEE-CENTRED LEARNING

Anthroposophical teaching model, 201

Audio-visual equipment, 171

Authoritative supervision, 266, 283

Basic teaching model, 197

Behavioural learning, 95, 202

Behavioural methodology, 232

Biodynamic methodology, 230

Cause-resolution approach, 236

Client-attachment, 248, 251, 255

Client-centred supervision, 289

Client-projection, 248, 250, 251, 253

Client-transference, 239, 248, 250, 251, 252, 254, 274, 275

Cognitive learning, 95

Cognitive methodology, 231

Cognitive-behavioural supervision, 291

Cognitive-focus approach, 237

Collegiate supervision, 265, 266, 268

Constructivist-interaction learning, 109

Context-based learning, 103

Co-operative supervision, 284

Course objectives, 21, 26, 38, 55, 57, 127, 136, 155

Course programme, 43, 46, 51, 53, 54, 55, 56, 57, 61, 62, 64, 69, 143, 147, 152, 155, 175

Course topics, 46, 55

Critical-appraisal learning, 107, 202

Critical-reflection learning, 108

Curriculum-centred teaching, 153

Cycle of learning experience model, 199

David Kolb, 199

Developmental supervision, 287, 288

Diversity learning, 109

Dreyfus model of skill acquisition, 85, 86

Educational psychology, 77, 143

Effect-resolution approach, 236

Emotive-focus approach, 237

Environmental-engagement learning, 106

Episodic learning, 151

Experiential learning, 78, 99, 199

Experimental learning, 118, 202

Formal assessment, 137, 139, 153, 184

Formative supervision, 264

General Hypnotherapy Register (GHR), 6

General Hypnotherapy Standards Council (GHSC), 5

Gestalt learning, 98

Group demonstration, 160, 162, 168, 171, 172, 174, 175

Group discussion, 162

Group presentation, 157, 159, 160, 168, 171, 174, 175, 181, 182

Group questioning, 157, 163, 164, 168, 183

Group supervision, 279, 280, 285, 286

Group tuition, 43

Handout material, 170, 171, 174, 175

Hubert Dreyfus, 85

Human-communication learning, 105

Humanistic learning, 98

Humanistic methodology, 228

Imitative-practice learning, 120

Individual supervision, 279, 280, 285

Individual tuition, 43

Informal assessment, 136, 192

Information processing learning. *See* CRITICAL-APPRAISAL LEARNING

Inspirational guidance, 220

Integrated-development supervision, 291

Internet resources, 174

Knowledge acquisition, 84, 182

Learner assessment, 71, 135, 137, 138, 193

Learner motivation, 123, 126

Learner rapport, 132

Learning activity, 22, 31, 61, 70, 71, 81, 88, 89, 90, 109, 115, 117, 123, 145, 148, 162, 200

Learning approach, 202

Learning environment, 13, 77, 103, 110, 149

Learning experience, 15, 26, 32, 33, 62, 79, 83, 84, 89, 93, 96, 99, 103, 108, 110, 111, 112, 115, 116, 117, 118, 119, 120, 121, 122, 124, 127, 129, 130, 131, 145, 147, 148, 149, 152, 158, 160, 166, 174, 176, 179, 183, 184, 187, 189, 190, 192, 194, 195, 198, 199, 200, 201, 202, 264

Learning objectives, 40, 143, 184, 185, 189, 191, 192, 194, 199, 203

Learning potential, 13, 22, 29, 32, 77, 125, 127, 129, 195

Learning process, 13, 26, 30, 31, 33, 37, 78, 79, 80, 88, 96, 99, 101, 110, 111, 123, 129, 149, 152, 153, 169, 175, 192, 198, 199, 200, 204

Learning strategy, 115, 116

Learning style, 115, 117, 121, 202

Learning-based learning, 93

Learning-based theory, 93

Lesson plan. *See* SESSION PLAN

Matrix-centred supervision, 290

Mentoring guidance, 219

Mission statement, 37, 38

Modular content, 61, 70

Module objectives, 64

Module topics, 62

Participative learning, 78

Participative supervision, 284

Passive learning process, 89, 90

Peer-support group supervision, 279

Perceptive learning, 120

Personal development, 162

Personal therapy, 14, 15, 16, 22

Personality-oriented learning. *See* SOCIAL-AWARENESS LEARNING

Person-centred supervision, 290

Practical guidelines, 183

Practical skill, 14, 16, 23, 33, 37, 61, 63, 70, 78, 81, 83, 85, 86, 88, 90, 91, 93, 94, 95, 96, 100, 101, 103, 104, 109, 110, 112, 115, 116, 117, 121, 122, 123, 124, 125, 126, 130, 131, 136, 138, 145, 147, 149, 151, 152, 153, 158, 161, 162, 164, 165, 168, 169, 175, 179,181, 182, 183, 184, 185, 186, 187, 197

Practitioner course, 23, 37, 38, 41, 51, 54, 60, 67, 74, 151

Practitioner training, 5, 24, 91, 152, 153, 264

Presentation equipment, 172

Presentation software, 171

Process-based learning, 83

Professional development, 9

Professional guidance, 217, 218, 222

Project-work, 166

Prospective trainee, 21, 23, 24, 25, 38

Psychodynamic methodology, 228

Psychodynamic supervision, 289

Psychotherapeutic supervision, 287

Reflective learning, 117, 199, 202

Restorative supervision, 265, 268

Robert Glaser, 197

Rudolf Steiner, 201

Scheme of work. *See* TRAINING PROGRAMME

Self-awareness learning, 97, 98, 202, 214

Session objectives, 41

Seven-phase supervisory approach, 274, 275

Situational-activity learning, 107

Skill acquisition, 85

Social-interaction learning, 105

State-oriented methodology, 229

Supervised practice, 86, 157, 164, 165, 168, 184

Supervisee counter-attachment, 259

Supervisee counter-projection, 257

Supervisee counter-transference, 257, 258

Supervisee-centred supervision, 289, 290

Supervisee-client interaction, 207, 245, 246, 248, 249, 251, 259, 267, 274, 275, 276, 287, 288, 290

Supervisory function, 207, 208, 221

Supervisory group, 280, 281, 282, 283, 284, 286

Supportive guidance, 218

Syllabus. *See* TRAINING PROGRAMME

Tangible outcomes, 183

Teaching activity, 29, 30, 63, 70, 77, 78, 83, 91, 123, 124, 135, 143, 144, 147, 157, 158, 160, 167, 171, 190, 191, 193, 198

Teaching methodology, 30, 32, 83, 84, 85, 86, 137, 189, 190, 192, 194

Teaching model, 197, 198, 201, 203, 204

Teaching resources, 169, 176

Teaching-learning plan. *See* SESSION PLAN

Theoretical knowledge, 14, 16, 23, 24, 25, 30, 33, 37, 61, 63, 71, 78, 81, 83, 84, 85, 88, 90, 91, 93, 95, 96, 100, 101, 103, 108, 109, 110, 112, 115, 116, 117, 119, 121, 122, 123, 124, 125, 126, 130, 138, 145, 147, 153, 159, 166, 169, 172, 175, 179, 181, 183, 184, 185, 186, 197, 225, 226, 235, 240, 246, 252

Theoretical learning, 48, 118, 144, 184, 202

Three-phase supervisory approach, 273

Tiered-development supervision, 292

Trainee feedback, 185

Trainee performance, 184

Trainee-centred learning, 78

Trainee-centred teaching, 152

Trainer motivation, 17

Training environment, 29, 30, 70, 126, 156

Training module, 53, 61, 62, 69

Training programme, 23, 31, 37, 43, 53, 60, 80, 126, 144, 157, 162, 163, 165, 171, 179, 189, 190, 191, 194, 218, 264

Training session, 39, 69, 70, 71, 72, 73, 74, 78, 80, 143, 170

Transpersonal methodology, 230

Treatment strategy, 238

Tutorial function, 77

About Jacquelyne Morison

Jacquelyne Morison is the founder and the course director of Jacquelyne Morison Hypnotherapy Training (JMHT).

JMHT provides hypnotherapy training courses for both prospective hypnotherapy-psychotherapy practitioners and for working professionals held in the UK and worldwide. Full details of all training courses can be found on the JMHT website (www.jmhypnotraining.co.uk).

Most importantly JMHT provides courses in Teaching and Training Skills and in Supervisory Skills for hypnotherapy trainers and alternative therapy practitioners from a range of therapeutic disciplines.

Jacquelyne is the author of *Creative Analytical Hypnotherapy* (2016), *Analytical Hypnotherapy Volume 1* (2010) and *Volume 2* (2009), *Psycho-Spiritual Therapy* (2019), *The Truly Dynamic Therapist* (2008) and *Hypnotic Art Therapy* (2014). She is also a chapter contributor to

Clinical Hypnosis Textbook: A Guide to Practical Intervention (2015) by Ursula James.

Jacquelyne has stacked up several decades of teaching experience in hypnotherapy training not only working under her own umbrella but also as the Principal Course Tutor for the International College of Eclectic Therapies (ICET) in London and as a visiting lecturer at the Institute of Clinical Hypnotherapy and Psychotherapy (ICHP) in the Republic of Ireland and in Germany.

Previously Jacquelyne was an information technology Training Consultant and a Business Studies Lecturer at which time she undertook teacher training and she was a chief examiner for the Joint Examining Board for Teachers' Diplomas for a number of years.

Jacquelyne has a BA in Clinical Hypnosis, a BMus and an MA in Music and holds a PGCE in post-compulsory education with special reference to hypnotherapy-psychotherapy training.

www.ingramcontent.com/pod-product-compliance
Lightning Source LLC
Chambersburg PA
CBHW040750020526
44118CB00042B/2831